CITIZENSHIP Today

Chris Culshaw
Jenny Wales
Paul Clarke
Neil Reaich

Success through qualifications

Published by HarperCollinsPublishers Limited

77–85 Fulham Palace Road

Hammersmith

London

W6 8JB

www.CollinsEducation.com
Online support for schools and colleges

First published 2002

Reprinted 10 9 8 7 6 5 4 3 2 1

ISBN: 0 00 713463 0

British Library Cataloguing in Publication Data

A Catalogue record for this publication is available from the British Library

Commissioned by Thomas Allain-Chapman

Project editor: Kate Haywood

Editor: Nancy Terry

Picture research: Suzanne Williams

Cover and internal design: Ken Vail Graphic Design, Cambridge

Cover photograph: Josef Peter Fankhauser/Getty Images/Stone

Production: Katie Morris

Printed and bound by Scotprint

Acknowledgements

HarperCollinsPublishers would like to thank the readers of this title, Anne Murray-Hudson, David Barrs and Nicholas Price, and Anthony Batchelor, Principal Examiner of Citizenship for Edexcel for his input as Consultant on this project.

The publishers would also like to thank the following for permission to reproduce photographs:

Action-Plus p 29t/Glyn Kirk; ©Amnesty International Publications, 1 Easton Street, London WC1X 0DJ, UK http://www.amnesty.org p 136tr, bl & br; Andes Press Agency/Carlos Reyes-Manzo pp 19b, 20cl, 024c, 62b; Patricia Briggs p 67bl & br; Bubbles Photo Library pp 12/John Powell, 44t/Jennie Woodcock, 45t/Amanda Knapp, 74bl/Ian West, 74br/Jennie Woodcock, 105/Jonathon Chappell, 106bl/Pauline Cutler, 96tr/Ian West; Courtesy of Carphone Warehouse p 102t; Courtesy of Claire Ward MP p 68c; Collections pp 19c/Nigel Hawkins, 19t/Bill Kirk, 20l/Brian Shuel, 36t/Ed Gabriel, 99b/Loz Simpson, 54tc/Nigel Hawkins; © Commission for Racial Equality p 30; Corbis pp 22/c Hulton-Deutsch Collection, 31/Paul A Souders, 34tr/Joseph Schwartz, 34tl/Bettman; Deryc Sands/Palace of Westminster Staff News pp 70b, 72; © Electoral Reform Society p 80; Courtesy of George Osborne MP p 68t; GettyOne Image Bank pp 112b/Dag Sundberg, 126/Real Life, 130/Tom Owen Edmunds; GettyOne Stone pp 26l/Ian Shaw, 26c/Peter Cade, 42b/Carin Krasner, 43/Marc Schlossman, 52tl/Chris Casaburi, 52tr/Joe McBride, 106cr/John Lamb, 90t/Walter Hodges, 106tl/Pierre Choiniere; GettyOne Telegraph pp 40t/Ryanstock, 27br/Steve Belkowitz; Greenpeace UK Photolibrary pp 77/Jeremy Sutton, 137/Daniel Beltra; Herman Miller p 128t; Hulton Getty Archive pp 41, 82; Jean-Marc Poilpré p 87 & 96tl; Jennifer Plucknett p 120b; John Walmsley pp 23, 27bl, 28, 56, 78l, 112t, 096bl; Kate Last p67t/Nancy Terry p 65l; NASA p 115t; PhotoDisc pp 40b/Brian McVay, 98/Ryan McVay, 49r/Doug Menuez; Photofusion pp 4l/Paul Baldesare, 8/Christa Stadtler, 9/Graham Burns, 14/David Tothill, 18tl/Peter Olive, 18bc/Bob Watkins, 18r/John Phillips, 20tr/Ian Simpson, 24tl/Paul Bigland, 24bl/Crispin Hughes, 24tr/Libby Welch, 24br/Paul Doyle, 26r/Paul Baldeare, 27tl, 27tr/David Montford, 32tl/Steve Eason, 37/Christa Stadtler, 38/David Tothill, 44b/Bob Watkins, 48/Christa Stadtler, 49l/G. Montgomery, 58/Mark Campbell, 59/Colin Edwards, 63/David Montford, 65r/Mark Campbell, 66/David Montford, 68b/Robert Brook, 74tr/Sally Lancaster, 74tl/Paul Doyle, 78c/Ute Klaphake, 78r/David Montford, 88/David Tothill, 102b/Sam Tanner, 115b/Ian Simpson, 114/Mark Campbell, 118/Robert Brook, 121t/Robert Brook, 123t/Bipinchandra Mistry, 123b/Ray Roberts, 6/Christa Stadtler, 54tr/Christa Stadtler, 54tl/G. Montgomery, 96tc/Paul Doyle, 96cl/Sally Lancaster, 60/Mark Campbell; Press Association pp 20br/William Conran, 25t/Paul Faith, 25b/Owen Humphreys, 32b/EPA, 34b/EPA, 39/Dave Kendall, 42t/Barry Batchelor, 46t/Paul Faith, 46b/Gareth Copley, 52b/Matthew Fearn, 53/Neil Munns, 57/Ben Curtis, 69/Andrew Parsons, 70t/Andy Butterton, Malcolm Croft, 81b/John Giles, 83/EPA, 85/PA, 86l/EPA, 86r/Toby Melville, 86c/Sean Dempsey, 90bl/Peter Jordan, 92/Louisa Butler, 99t/Andy Butterton, 103/John Giles, 109/EPA, 124/EPA, 125r/EPA, 128b/Phil Noble, 133t/EPA, 134l/Toby Melville, 135/EPA, 81t/Matthew Fearn, 132t, 132b, 6/Ben Curtis, 54bcr/Owen Humphreys, 54bcl/Neil Munns, 73/Andy Butterton, 96br/Ben Curtis; Rank Xerox p 120tr; Remarkable pencils p 120tl; Science Photo Library p 45b/James Holmes/Celltech Ltd; © Sky News p 90br; Still Pictures pp 4r/Mike Jackson, 4b/Mark Edwards, 32tr, 33/Tim Page, 36b/Nick Cobbing, 108t/Jorgen Schytte, 110t/Dylan Garcia, 110b/Peter Frischmuth, 111/Mark Edwards, 113/Hartmut Schwarzbach, 116/Mark Edwards, 117t/McCallion-UNEP, 121b/Hartmut Schwarzbach, 122/Dylan Garcia, 125bl/Frans Lemmens, 125tl/Paul Glendell, 133b/Hartmut Schwarzbach, 6/Jorgen Schytte, 54bc/Tim Page, 108b/Jorgen Schytte; UNAIDS p 134r; Village AID p 117b; Young & Powerful p 29b/Northcliffe Newspaper

The publishers gratefully acknowledge the following for permission to reproduce copyright material. Every effort has been made to trace copyright holders, but in some cases this has proved impossible. The publishers would be happy to hear from any copyright holder that has not been acknowledged.

Thanks to: Article 12 (article12.com) for the information on the Rights of the Child; ASDA for the extract from the Colleague Handbook; the CREATE Project, Liverpool; Greenpeace: website letter; The Guardian: 'Ford's president signs pact' by Seumas Milne & David Gow, 26 Oct 1999, '£60,000 for blind teacher' by Rebecca Smithers, 5 July 2000 and 'Single mother wins case' by Linus Gregoriadis, 3 August 1999; Chris North (chrisnorth69@hotmail.com) and International Campaign to Ban Mines (www.icbl.org) for the poem 'Two Steps'; Herts County Council for the image from www.hertsdirect.org/youth website; HMSO for the figures on firework injuries Oct–Nov 1999 (DTI), figures on population of Great Britain by ethnic group 1998 (ONS), Noise complaints to EHOs (DEFRA 2001) and Safer Journeys to School (DETR website 1999); Hull County Council for the image from their website; Kick it Out 2001 (published by KIO, PO Box 29544, London, EC2A 4WR) for the extract 'Racism in football'; Rank Xerox for the photograph and caption; Remarkable Pencils (www.remarkable.com) for the photograph of pencils, and Friends of the Earth for the caption; Suffolk County Council for their website material 'Graffiti wall'; the European Communities for their web page

Illustrations: Nick Duffy, Tony Forbes and Kathryn Prewett

Contents

What is Citizenship?

1. Look at each of the pictures on these two pages. Write down the problems that each one shows.

2. What could be done to help overcome each problem?

3. Who do you think should be responsible for solving the problems?

What's involved?

The issues in the pictures cover some of the areas of Citizenship which you will work on through the course. All the images show different aspects of life and suggest ways in which people might find themselves in difficulties – both big and small. For example:

- if the local cinema closes, it may be a pain but there is likely to be another one fairly near
- if nobody buys the coffee you grow, finding another way of life will be difficult
- if you use a wheelchair and there are no ramps beside steps, you will face problems
- if people are messing up your local environment, who will have to pay the price?
- laws are made to try to make life better for everyone – but some people break them
- you might need a new school or hospital where you live but the Government may not choose to spend its money that way.

Citizenship is about learning to live together as a community, both within your own country and beyond. Citizenship education gives people the knowledge they need to play a full part in society. Understanding how society works will help you to live better within it, and give you the power to make things better for other people, too.

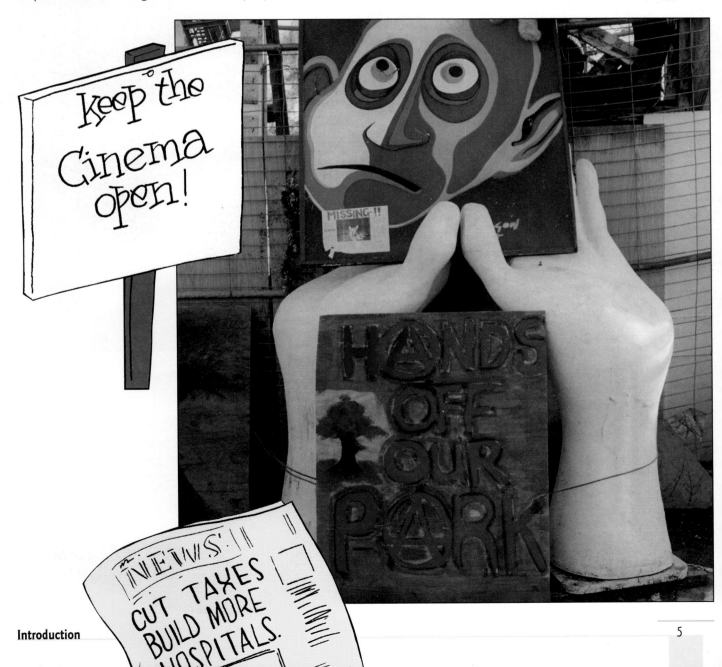

Your Citizenship Studies course

Citizenship Today

This course explores citizenship issues, and helps you to understand your role and how you can be involved.

There are two parts to the course – **Citizenship Today** and **Participating in Society**.

Citizenship Today is divided into three themes:

Theme 1
Human rights

This theme explores different communities in the UK. It shows that respect and understanding between people helps create a better society. You will look at people's rights and responsibilities as individuals, consumers and employees. You will also learn about why laws are needed and the kinds of laws that protect citizens.

Theme 2 Power, politics and the media

This theme shows how you can make a change to society, both as an individual and as a member of voluntary groups. You will learn how you can speak to your local council about issues that concern you. A section on political power shows how you can make a difference by voting in elections. You will find out about how people can get involved in pressure groups.

This theme also looks at the power of the media in today's society.

Theme 3
The global village

In this section, you will learn about how the economy works and how it affects everyone. You will find out about how business affects our lives, both in the UK and in the rest of the world.

Other global issues are looked at in a section on the environment, which focuses on environmental problems and offers some possible solutions.

Finally, you will learn about some international organizations, like the European Union and the United Nations, and find out what they do. You will also read about international pressure groups, like Greenpeace, and discover how you can join in their work.

The exam

The assessment has two parts to match the two parts of the course.

Edexcel Citizenship today

Written paper
1 hour 15 minutes   60% of total marks

Section A	This examines your **Citizenship activity**. You will: ● answer short-answer questions about your **Citizenship activity** ● write a long answer about your **Citizenship activity**.
Section B	This examines your understanding of the **Content**. You will: ● be given a variety of information sources, e.g. short texts, graphs and pictures to do with **ONE** of the Themes from the **Content** ● answer short-answer questions about the information you have been given.
Section C	This examines your understanding of the **Content**. You will: ● answer short-answer questions on **ALL** the themes from the **Content** ● write a long answer to **ONE** question you can choose from **ONE** of the Themes.

The Citizenship Activity

Participating in Society

Internal assessment portfolio
40% of total marks

You have to take part in a **Citizenship Activity**. As well as doing the activity you have to:

● describe how you planned the activity
● write about how you carried it out
● provide evidence of your activity and how you went about it
● describe how well you thought it went and whether you think it was a useful **Citizenship Activity**.

When you hand in your portfolio it needs to contain:

● a **Front sheet** saying what the activity is
● a four-page **Response form** with these sections:
● **Section one: Planning**
● **Section two: Activity log**
● **Section three: Communication with supporting evidence**
● **Section four: Evaluation.**

Sections one and four don't have to be written. You can do a spoken presentation of these sections, but you must be able to prove that you did the presentation.

The following pages will show you how to carry out your **Citizenship Activity** for **Participating in Society**.

The Citizenship Activity – what shall we do?

What activity?

Your Citizenship Studies course asks you to take part in a Citizenship activity, keep a record of how it works and decide how well it all went. You may already be involved in activities that fit the bill, but if not, you'll need to work out what to do. There are all sorts of alternatives:

- Is there an open space that could be turned into a garden or some other sort of community or school resource?

- Are there some elderly people who would enjoy a regular visit?

- Can you help some younger people with their reading?

- Could you work with other young people to discuss community issues like graffiti, vandalism or services that you would like to see in your area?

- Can you carry out a project while on work experience?

- Do you have a school council?

- Could you organize a school event?

- Could you find out about employment rights and responsibilities when you do your work experience?

- Does your school have a radio station? Could you start one up?

- Why not run a mock election, a mock trial or hold an international organization's meeting?

- How about organizing a petition, opinion poll or display about something you care about?

- Could you run a mini-enterprise?

All these ideas can be put to use. Being involved in something that really interests you always makes it easier. For example, does the environment mean something to you? Perhaps you are worried about crime in your area. Or do you want more facilities for young people in the area?

If your activity is based on work experience, you will need to think carefully about what you want to find out. How about rights and responsibilities of people in the workplace? Or you might investigate how the business is affected by consumer protection laws.

If you are making things or providing a service – like doing refreshments at the school fair – you might turn it into a mini-enterprise. This would mean deciding on the costs of all the things you need and thinking about the price you can charge. You would need to do some research into this. How would you market your product? How much profit do you aim to make? How will you use the profits to benefit your school or community?

Working in a team

The Citizenship Studies course expects you to work as part of a team. The team may be made up of your school friends or it may be a group outside school. It is important to think about the contribution you and the others make to the activity.

Make sure that everyone has a role in the activity. It makes it much easier to identify each person's contribution if you can explain their area of responsibility.

Action

Sit down with a blank sheet of paper and think about what you want to do.

1 Start by writing down all your ideas.
2 List all the advantages and disadvantages of each idea.
3 Put them in order from best to worst.
4 Is the one at the top the one you really want to carry out? If so, go ahead. If not, have another look at the list.

Check point

■ Before you make a final decision, check with your teacher that your activity is suitable for your exam requirements.

■ You will describe and analyse the contribution you and the others in your group make in the exam and in your **Response form** in your portfolio, so it's a good idea to think about this right from the start of your activity.

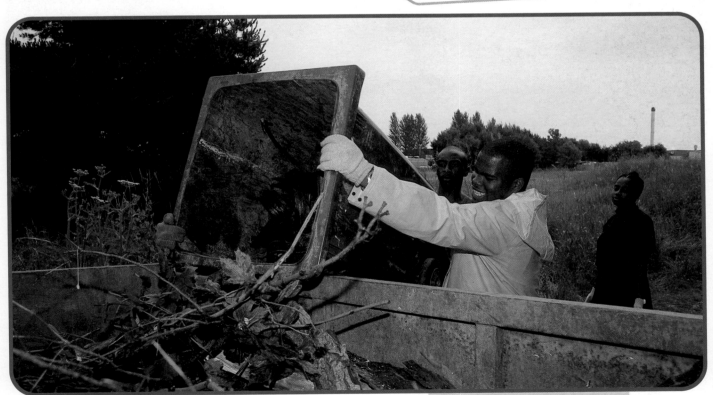

1 Make a list of the contributions you think people will have to make to plan and carry out this activity.
2 Why do you think the activity is good for Citizenship Studies?
3 Which part of the course does it relate to? See page 6.

A group of students clears a corner of the school grounds to create a garden.

Planning the activity

The steps to success

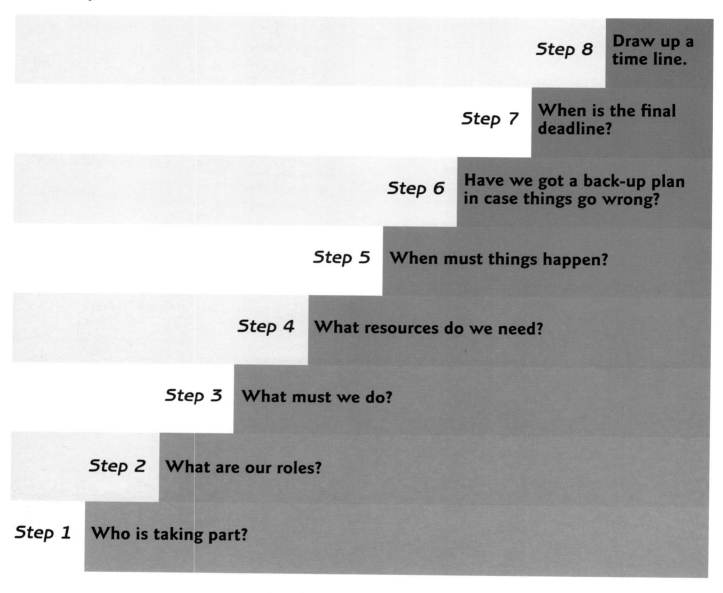

Step 8 Draw up a time line.

Step 7 When is the final deadline?

Step 6 Have we got a back-up plan in case things go wrong?

Step 5 When must things happen?

Step 4 What resources do we need?

Step 3 What must we do?

Step 2 What are our roles?

Step 1 Who is taking part?

Planning

Planning means setting out what must be done and making sure that everyone knows their responsibilities. By following the steps above, you will be on the right track. You will need to end up with two documents. The first document will be:

A list of group members and their responsibilities
Brainstorm all the things that need to be done. Do they fall into groups? Who has the skills needed for each activity? Should people work in pairs or on their own?

Then, when you have made the decisions, draw up your list which explains exactly what everyone has to do. Make sure you keep the list safe. You will need it to check whether everything has been done and to put in your records. This will lead to the second document you need, which is:

A time line showing what must be done and when
Once you have gathered all the information you need and put your plans together, you can draw up a time line. Put the name of the person responsible beside every point. This will give you markers to check whether everything is on track. It will also give everyone target dates for getting things done. Remember – gathering information can take time so make it a priority.

October 1

Set up enterprise

Allocate roles

Decide on the product

Decide on materials needed

Find suppliers and prices of materials

October 7

£
£

Work out costs

Work out expected price

Order supplies

Think about marketing

December 3

Present financial information

Work out amount of money to be given to charity

October 21

Start production

Plan marketing

November 28

School fair

Sell products

Collect revenue from sales

FOR SALE

November 7

Start marketing

BUY OUR CAKES!

Check point ✔

Response form
Section one: Planning

You need to show how you planned your activity in Section one of your **Response form**. You can use the 'List of members of the group and their responsibilities', and the 'Time line' to show this.

You can also describe how you set up the activity by doing a presentation. If you do this you still need to provide **supporting evidence** of the presentation, for example, transparencies or a PowerPoint presentation you used (probably of the group members' list and the time line) or statements from people who heard your presentation.

Action

When you have decided on your activity, get together with the rest of the team and work out how you are going to go about planning and putting your ideas into action.

Gathering the evidence

Keeping track

While you are carrying out your Citizenship Activity, you need to keep careful records of everything you do. This will include an **Activity log** and a collection of **supporting evidence**. They will both build a picture of what you did and how you did it. Gathering all the information as you go along will help you to put it all together. It's very easy to forget exactly what happened when!

In the **Activity log**, you will record everything you take part in, such as meetings, research, presentations, or anything else that contributes to your activity. At each stage you should explain what you are trying to achieve. If you have changed your plans at any point, these changes should be included and explained. You should also record who else was involved in each event and when it took place.

1 How are these students showing their Citizenship skills?
2 What do you think they had to do to plan this activity?
3 What sort of evidence do you think they collected for their portfolio?
4 How does their activity relate to the content of the course?

Activity log

Activity	Group/individual	Date
Meeting with teacher at local primary school to discuss arrangements for giving reading support to Year 2 children. Programme set to start from 22 Jan. Ms Osborne gave guidance on helping with reading.	Ms Ann Osborne (teacher) Paul West Suzanna Giuliani Rajesh Golcha Kate Ridley	8 Jan
Team meeting to discuss plans and share ideas on working with the children.	Paul West Suzanna Giuliani Rajesh Golcha Kate Ridley	15 Jan
First session with children. The team each worked with three children. Ms Osborne gave feedback to help next time.	Ms Ann Osborne Paul West Suzanna Giuliani Rajesh Golcha Kate Ridley	22 Jan

Check point ✔

Response form
Section two: Activity log

You need to include the **Activity log** for Section two of your **Response form**. It should show how the activity relates to issues covered in the **Content** of the course. You should include details of how individuals, and the group as a whole, contributed to the activity.

Supporting evidence

There are all sorts of ways in which you can submit your **supporting evidence**. It doesn't just have to be in writing. You need to provide at least one piece of evidence and no more than four. Just submitting an agenda for a meeting isn't really enough. You would need some other evidence as well. If the work is all written, it should be between 500 and 1000 words. There are all sorts of ways of recording your activity. Here are some suggestions:

- PowerPoint slides
- videos
- CD-Roms
- letters
- photographs
- banners
- web pages
- audio or written records of presentation work
- extended written work
- questionnaires
- agendas or minutes of meetings.

A video which showed the extent of your activity would be fine. A tape of a meeting or a presentation about you carrying out your activity would also give a clear picture of how you were working. If you used PowerPoint or some other presentation software to explain or persuade people of your point of view, it would make a good piece of evidence.

Perhaps you made a website to let people know what you were up to. This would be helpful evidence as it will show just what you were trying to do and how you went about it.

If you've been investigating what people want or think, you may have used a questionnaire. This, together with the results, would make a good piece of evidence as it would show the way you worked and what you found out.

Did you write a document that was used to explain, persuade or justify what you were up to? This would form a useful piece of evidence as it would give people a good picture of the activity.

Check point ✔

Response form
Section three: Communication with supporting evidence

For this section of the **Response form** you have to list all the materials and sources you have used as your **supporting evidence**. You should describe how each piece of evidence helped you do the activity. For example, an agenda of a meeting helped you plan a particular stage of your activity, or a questionnaire helped you get information about your activity.

Evaluation

Did I make a difference?

What about other people?

Did we achieve our objectives?

Did it all go according to plan?

What did others think?

How did our activity make a difference to other people?

Did you make a difference?

When your activity has been completed, there are just two things left to do:

1 Weigh up your contribution

Look back at everything you did. Did you have a leadership role? Did you help to keep people on track? Were you are good team member? Did you have an effect on outsiders? Did you suggest changes in the plan? Would you have done anything differently? How do you think others viewed your contribution? Could you have done more?

2 Weigh up the contribution of others

Who were the main contributors? How did they contribute? Were they good team members? Were some people more important than others? Why? Did one person have an effect on others? Were there difficult moments or low points?

Your answers to the questions above will depend on the sort of activity you took part in. For example:

- if your group was involved in helping younger children with their reading, did you feel they enjoyed it and that you helped their reading to progress?

- if your group ran a mini-enterprise, did you make sure people didn't spend too much on making the product?
- if your group was trying to persuade the local council to provide more sports facilities, did you manage to get a report in the local paper or on local radio?
- would you do things differently another time?

Exam check

Response form
Section four: Evaluation

This is the last section of the **Response form**. This is where you write up your thoughts about everybody's contribution to the activity and say how successful you thought it was. Was there any point at which you could have done things differently? Could you have done things better?

You can also do a spoken presentation of your evaluation of the activity, but you must provide **supporting evidence** that you have done it.

Summary of Participating in Society

Your portfolio will include the following:

● a **Front sheet** describing the activity

● a four-page **Response form** with these sections:

- **Section one: Planning**
- **Section two: Activity log**
- **Section three: Communication with supporting evidence**
- **Section four: Evaluation**

Sections one and four don't have to be written. You can do a spoken presentation of these sections, but you must be able to prove that you did the presentation.

Your teacher will give you with the **Response form** to fill in. There isn't a lot of space on it so keep your thoughts simple and straightforward. You will probably want to write it in rough before you fill it in.

At the end of the course

Like all other GCSEs, there is an exam at the end. One part is based on your **Citizenship Activity**. First of all you will be asked to review the work you have done in your activity. Then you will be posed a question that relates it to the rest of the Citizenship course. The example on the right shows the sorts of thing you might be asked to do.

You can use all the things you have been thinking about for your **Response form** to help you answer these questions. For example, would the activity have worked if one person had been working alone? Was one person really effective in the activity? This all fits in with teamwork and leadership.

By now you will know whether your aims were realistic. If you achieved them, they probably were. Was someone influential in deciding on the aims? Were the aims the product of the whole group? Did you have to change your plans?

Remember – the exam will ask you to consider another point of view. You won't get many marks if you don't!

Think about the successes and difficulties you and others experienced during your Citizenship Activity.

Do you agree with the view that 'one person can make a difference'?

Give reasons for your opinion, showing you have considered another point of view.

You could include the following points in your answer and other information of your own.

● Teamwork

● Leadership

● Choosing realistic aims.

Theme 1 Human rights

What is a community?

Objective

Understand the meaning of community and that people can belong to more than one community at the same time.

Getting you thinking

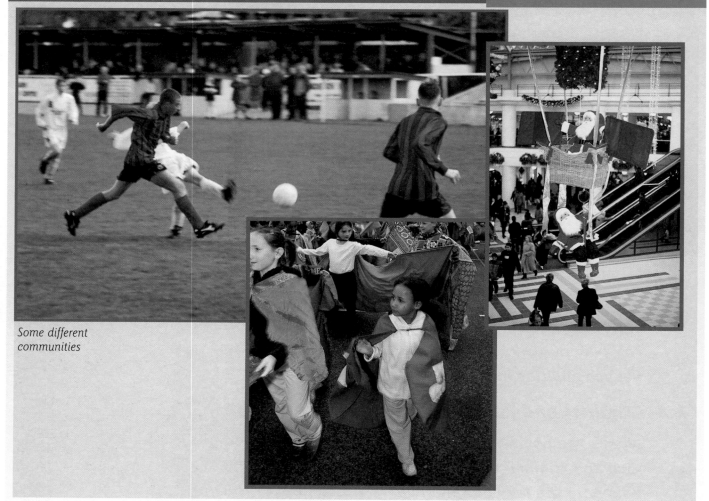

Some different communities

1 How many of these **communities** do you belong to?

2 How many of these communities do you share with people of different ages and/or interests?

3 If you don't belong to some of these communities, do you know people who do? How do you know these people?

4 What do these communities give you and what do you give them?

Belonging to a community

A community is a group of people who are connected in some way. Most people belong to several communities. Someone your age, living in the UK, could be a member of several communities – school, local neighbourhood, the country, the European Union, a religious group, and others.

Neighbourhoods

There is a lot of overlap between different communities.

A **neighbourhood** community refers to those people who share local interests because of where they live. It might be the whole of a village or small town but in a city the neighbourhood can be more difficult to identify. For example, someone living in Whitechapel in London might think of the neighbourhood as 'London', 'Whitechapel', 'the East End' or even their own particular street.

'I belong to ... '

As well as belonging to a neigbourhood, people are also connected by their lifestyle, religion, ethnicity or nationality.

Irish travellers

There are about 1300 Irish travellers in Northern Ireland. They are a centuries-old ethnic group which travels around in mobile homes. They have their own culture, customs, traditions and language.

The Chinese community

The Chinese community in the UK dates back to the mid-1800s. They live in all parts of the UK and there are well established 'Chinatowns' in Birmingham, Liverpool, London, Manchester and Newcastle. There are over 400 Chinese organizations that serve the needs of the Chinese community in the UK, including language schools, women's groups, and art and business associations. Chinese New Year, food, martial arts, medicine and feng shui have all become part of British life.

The Christian community

There are almost 49000 Christian churches in the United Kingdom, across more than 10 different denominations, ranging from Church of England to Roman Catholic, Methodist to Greek Orthodox. As well as involving people in the wider Christian community, many local churches are a focus for local people, offering facilities and events open to Christians and non-Christians alike.

The Muslim community

Almost all of the Muslim population in Britain are descendants of the families of people who came to Britain in the 1950s, 60s and 70s. However, Islam has been followed in Britain for centuries. At least 300 years ago Indian-Muslim sailors, recruited by the East India company, settled in port towns. The first mosque in Britain probably opened in Cardiff in 1860. Today, there are Muslim communities all over Britain.

Check your understanding

1 Explain why people can belong to more than one community and why there is an overlap between communities.

2 Describe what each of the four communities shown has in common. What makes each one a community?

Discuss

"It is easier to feel part of a community if you live in a village or small town compared to a city." Do you agree with this statement? Give reasons.

Key terms

community: a group of people in close contact and who share common interests and values

neighbourhood: a local area within which people live as neighbours, sharing living space and interests

A national culture

Objective

Understand the meaning of national identity and culture, and that Britain is a multicultural country.

1 These images are all associated with British culture. What images would you add?

What does it mean to be British?

This is a difficult question and it has many possible answers. Does it mean:

- you share a geographical boundary with other British people?
- you share a history that links the separate parts of England, Wales, Scotland and Northern Ireland?
- you share a common language?
- you identify with many common habits, values and pastimes?
- you have the right to have a British passport so you can move freely in and out of the United Kingdom?

A national identity is often easier to describe when you are in a different country. How might you feel if you went abroad on holiday? In Spain, for example, you would come across a different language, a different kind of diet, different kinds of schooling, different games played by children and adults.

A sense of belonging

A sense of belonging comes from growing up and living in a particular place. Parents, schools and the media pass on common ideas of British culture. Different generations are also influenced by their own personal experiences.

People who have fought in wars for their country are likely to feel a different sense of belonging from those who only feel British when they are away on holiday.

Which community?

People may also identify with different kinds of national community. People from ethnic minorities may feel more comfortable with members of their own ethnic community than with other **British nationals**. Similarly, people from the various regions such as the Midlands or the South West might identify more with people from their own region than others.

It is possible to belong to many different communities at the same time. Sports fans may feel quite comfortable supporting a British team in one competition, an English or Welsh team in another, and their local team in a third.

Population of Great Britain by ethnic group 2000–01 in millions	
White	53.0
Black Caribbean	0.5
Black African	0.4
Indian	1.0
Pakistani	0.7
Bangladeshi	0.3
Chinese	0.1
Other groups	1.1

Social Trends 2002, ONS

A multicultural community

The ethnic mix of the national community has changed steadily over the years to include a significant number of people of Afro-Caribbean, African and Asian descent. In some areas, the majority of the local population are now of one of these groups. In a **multicultural community**:

▶ a local school may serve a community with several different home languages and different festivals to celebrate

▶ welfare services often provide information printed in several languages

▶ hospitals and clinics work with a variety of traditions and expectations surrounding births and deaths

▶ local councils have to take account of different community needs for shops and religious buildings

▶ businesses may have staff and customers from a range of cultural backgrounds.

Check your understanding

1 What does it mean to say that Britain is a multicultural community?

2 List as many different aspects of British culture as you can which help define British national identity.

Discuss

Are there any instances when you feel more in common with one community than another?

Find out

What do your friends and family mean by 'being British'? Share your findings with the class.

Key terms

British nationals: citizens of the United Kingdom

multicultural community: a community made up of people from many different cultural or ethnic groups

Where are your roots?

Getting you thinking

Tom = Sharon

Baz = Tina   Michael   Kim = Sarah

Abby   Jordan   Ben   Jenni

"To forget your ancestors is to be a tree without roots" – Chinese proverb

1 If you traced your family tree, what kind of roots would it have?

2 Do you think it is important for you to know your roots? Give reasons.

A pick-and-mix people

Throughout its history, people have settled in Britain from many different countries. They bring their language, ideas and customs, all of which have mixed together to make up the country's culture.

Warlike invasions of Saxons, Vikings, Romans and Normans were followed by peaceful migrations from Europe and many former British colonies. Just look in the dictionary, phone book or map to find words and names from many languages.

In the past 250 years, about six million people have come from Ireland in search of a better life. Many came to the UK during the potato famine of the 1840s.

In 1860, one-quarter of the population of Liverpool were Irish migrants.

Poles have lived here since the reign of Queen Elizabeth I, but the majority of UK Poles settled here after World War II when Poland was occupied first by the Nazis, and then by the Soviet armies.

There has been a Jewish population in the UK for hundreds of years, but most arrived in the 1930s and 40s. They came to the UK to escape from religious and racial persecution in Russia and Eastern Europe.

In the 1950s, many people from British colonies in Africa, Asia and the Caribbean settled in the UK looking for work, as there was a shortage of manual and semiskilled employees in Britain during this period.

In the 1970s, thousands of Ugandan Asians arrived here after being expelled from Uganda.

Today **immigration** is more restricted.

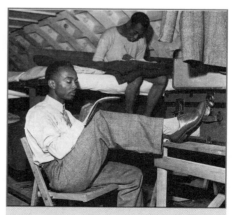

Two Jamaican immigrants write home in 1948. They had arrived at Tilbury Docks, London, from Jamaica in search of work.

Ethnic minorities in each region

UK average 7%

Scotland 2%

Northern Ireland 2%

North-East 2%

Yorkshire and Humberside 6%

North-West 4%

East Midlands 10%

West Midlands 5%

East 4%

Wales 2%

England 8%

South-East 3%

South-West 2%

London 25%

ONS 2001

Comings and goings: migration in and out of the UK 1971–2000		
Year	Immigration (000s)	Emigration (000s)
1971	200	240
1981	153	232
1991	337	264
2000	450	268

Check your understanding

1 Suggest two reasons why the UK is a culturally diverse society.

2 Why did many immigrants come to Britain in the 1950s?

3 In which regions, outside London, would you find the most culturally diverse communities?

4 What has happened to immigration and **emigration** in recent years?

5 Describe two things the council did to improve race relations in Leicester.

6 Do you think other regions of the UK will become more culturally diverse in future? Give reasons.

Find out

Research the background and culture of any immigrant groups that have settled in your local area. Find out why they left their homelands, and to what extent they have been able to retain their language and culture. Present your findings to the class.

Discuss

In pairs, list some ways in which the UK has benefited from immigrants, and some ways in which immigrants have benefited from their host community.

Leicester: a lesson in racial understanding

Many people living in Leicester have non-white roots, and Leicester is proud of of its **cultural diversity**. However, in the 1970s it was labelled one of the most racist cities in Britain. There were adverts in the local papers telling immigrants not to come to Leicester and racial tension was high.

The city council took the lead by outlawing racism. It promoted Leicester as a city that welcomes everybody. The council created Britain's first-ever race relations committee. A public education programme made people aware of others' hopes and fears. Since then, various groups have worked hard to promote good race relations in the city.

There are now over 1500 Asian businesses in the city, and in 2001 there were 13 Asian councillors on the city council. Festivals such as Diwali now attract over 25 000 people to the city.

Key terms

cultural diversity: the range of different groups that make up a wider population

emigration: leaving your homeland to live in another country

immigration: moving to another country to live there

Religious understanding

Objective

Understand the religious diversity of the UK and the importance of religious tolerance.

Getting you thinking

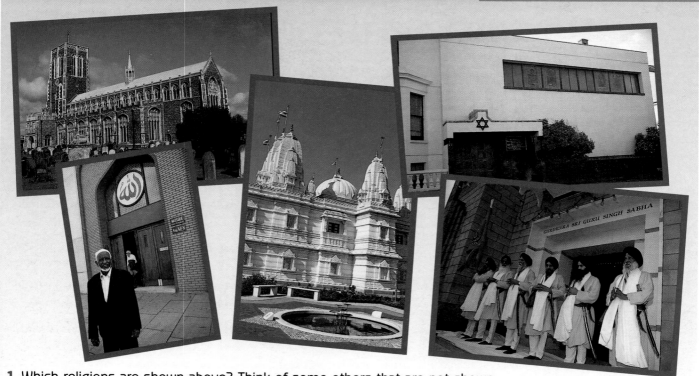

1 Which religions are shown above? Think of some others that are not shown.

2 List things all these religions have in common.

Diverse views

Although most UK citizens would probably claim to be Christians, there are many other diverse religious groups in the UK. Most of these are found in large cities, such as London, Birmingham, Manchester and Leeds, where most of the UK's ethnic **minority** communities live. This religious diversity is the result of people settling here over many years, mostly from former British colonies.

The main ethnic minority groups and their religions are:

Bangladeshis	Mostly Muslim (small number of Hindu)
Indians (Punjabis)	Mostly Sikh, some Hindus
Indians (Gujeratis)	Mostly Hindu, some Muslims
Pakistanis	Muslim
Chinese	Christian, Confucian and Buddhist
Afro-Caribbeans	Christian and Rastafarian

Religions of UK citizens with Indian roots

Sometimes an individual's clothes, or the food they eat, or the language they speak gives you a clue to their religion. But this is not always the case. For example, some UK citizens with Indian roots are Sikhs, but there are many others.

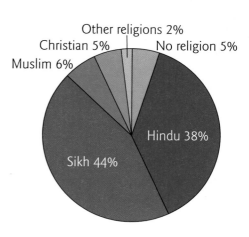

Other religions 2%
Christian 5%
No religion 5%
Muslim 6%
Hindu 38%
Sikh 44%

Within many religions there are different 'branches'. Anglicans, Methodists, Quakers and Catholics are all part of the wider Christian tradition but practise their religion in different ways. In the same way, Orthodox and Reform Jews share many beliefs but worship in separate synagogues.

All we wanted was to get our kids to school

3 September 2001

Hundreds of riot police and armed soldiers lined the road. They stood between the Protestants, who were shouting threats and abuse, and the Catholic girls and their parents. The girls, aged four to eleven, were on their way to Holy Cross school – a Catholic school in the middle of a Protestant housing estate. A mother of a six-year-old girl said, "It was terrifying. They were shouting 'Dirty tramps. Your kids are animals.' It was like walking into a wall of hate. I didn't think there was so much hate."

At the end of the school day, the girls left the school by a rear entrance and were taken home in taxis.

> ? What do the Holy Cross incident and Bradford attack have in common? What differences are there?

ASIAN YOUTHS ATTACK CHURCH

6 November 2001, Bradford

Police are looking for a gang of Asian youths who tried to set fire to a church on Bonfire Night. When the vicar chased the youths away, they stoned his car. After the police arrived, the youths ran off.

After this happened, local Muslims went to a service at the church and, at the end, they spoke to the congregation to express their 'deep regrets'. Also, a joint Christian/Muslim fund-raising group has been set up to raise money for people in Afghanistan.

Everyone's right

The United Nations (UN), an international organization to which most countries belong, put together a Declaration of Human Rights (see pages 32–33). It includes a section on religion, which means everyone is free to follow any religion or none. You have the right to join an established religion, or to start a sect or cult of your own. Nobody should be prevented from following a religion of their choice.

UN logo

Check your understanding

1 Why does the UK have such a diversity of religions? Can you name any other countries where you find the same religious diversity?

2 What does the Universal Declaration of Human Rights say about your religious freedoms? Is it always carried out?

Discuss

1 All world religions stress the importance of peace and **tolerance**, but there are sometimes tensions between people who belong to different religious groups. Why?

2 Suggest ways of improving religious understanding and tolerance between young people of different religions.

Key terms

minority: a small part of a larger group of people

tolerance: open-mindedness, acceptance

Identities

Objective

Understand the meaning of identity and some of the factors which determine it.

Getting you thinking

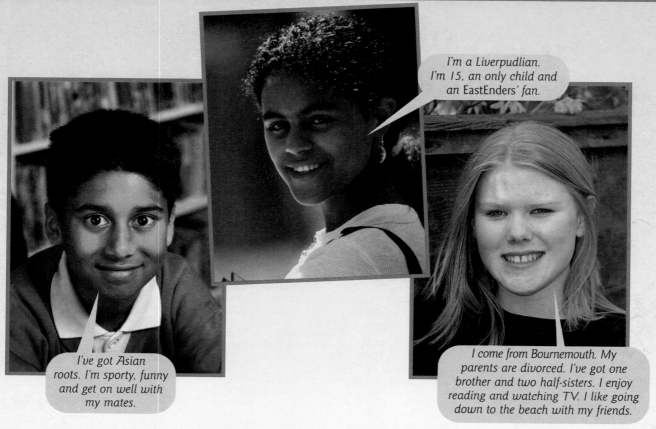

I'm a Liverpudlian. I'm 15, an only child and an EastEnders' fan.

I've got Asian roots. I'm sporty, funny and get on well with my mates.

I come from Bournemouth. My parents are divorced. I've got one brother and two half-sisters. I enjoy reading and watching TV. I like going down to the beach with my friends.

1 What has contributed to the identity of each of these people?

2 How do you think these factors have affected them?

3 How much does your identity depend on where you live? On your family's roots? On your religion?

4 If you had been asked the question, "Who are you?" when you were five years old, what would you have said? How would you answer this question now?

5 Make a list of factors that will shape your identity as you get older.

Who am I?

In some countries, such as France, all citizens must carry an **identity card**. This card gives details such as their name, address and date of birth.

The word '**identity**' has another, broader meaning. People's identity is a combination of where they come from and the influences on their lives.

Your identity develops and changes as you develop and change. Can you remember how you felt when you first went to school? You've learned a lot about yourself in the ten or

more years since then. You now have a better understanding of your good and bad points; you are more self-aware and better aware of how other people see you. Looking back, that five-year-old 'you' will seem like a very different person. Your identity will continue to develop further as you grow older and as you become an employee, partner/wife/ husband, parent, etc.

An identity card can't show all this information about you. Some governments like them because it means that people can be easily identified.

Conflicting loyalties

Britain has one of the highest rates of mixed-race (**dual heritage**) relationships in the world. By 2010 it is estimated that London will be made up of more dual heritage and black people than white. Whilst most people would agree that cultural diversity is a good thing, the mixing of races and nationalities can occasionally produce conflicts.

If, for example, your mother is Chinese, your father Irish and you were born in Paris but live in London, how would you answer the question: "Where are you from?"

If a Catholic marries a Muslim, what religion should their children belong to?

If your mother is German and your father is English, who should you support in the World Cup?

How do you react if someone tells you you're not really black and you're not really white?

? In your own words, describe the conflicting loyalties felt by each of the four people.

? Which person has the most difficult situation to resolve, and why?

? Suggest other situations which involve conflicting loyalties.

Check your understanding

What does 'dual heritage' mean? Describe how dual heritage can sometimes lead to conflicts of identity.

Discuss

"People are more alike than different." Agree or disagree? Give reasons.

Key terms

dual heritage: people with parents or ancestors of different origins

identity: who or what something is

identity card: a card that establishes someone's identity

Human rights

Meeting barriers

Getting you thinking

Some children were playing on the beach when an old 'bag lady' came along. She was talking to herself and picking things up off the beach as she walked. Parents called their children over and told them stay close by, until the old woman had moved on. The following day, they discovered that the old woman came to the beach every day, picking up bits of glass so children wouldn't cut their feet.

1 Why did the parents call their children over? What is the moral of the story?

2 Have you ever misjudged somebody because of their dress or behaviour? Have you ever been misjudged?

3 Think of individuals or groups who are misjudged in this way, and say why they have been misunderstood.

The sliding scale of discrimination

persecution
making people suffer because they are different

discrimination
treating people differently for unjust reasons

prejudice
thinking unfairly

Prejudice and discrimination

People treat each other badly for all sorts of reasons. Such unfair treatment can mean that people don't get jobs or are kept out of clubs, as well as many other things. The case studies here show some strategies used to overcome prejudice and discrimination.

Part of the 'rough and tumble' of schooling?

In spring 2000, Lancaster Youth and Community Service set up a group for gay and lesbian youngsters, to help them cope with the **homophobic** bullying they encountered in schools and colleges. One young man who belongs to the group said, "I love coming here. It's the only time in the week I feel completely safe. It's the one place I can be myself."

? What does the young man's comment tell you about homophobic bullying?

? What can schools do to reduce homophobic bullying?

28

'Education is the answer'

Although there are many black and Asian football players and they are accepted by football fans everywhere, there are still problems with racial prejudice and discrimination. Some fans have been known to call out racist comments and make monkey noises when black players are on the pitch.

Sir Alex Ferguson, Manchester United's manager, is a supporter of football's anti-**racism** campaign, 'Kick It Out!'. This is what he says:

"I think it's all down to education and how people are brought up. I was brought up in a family where there was never any prejudice. I think education from family and school is the most important thing. If parents are saying to their kids 'Don't play with that Charlie down the road because he is black', what message does that give? I think education is the secret."

? Do you agree with Sir Alex that 'it's all down to education'? Give reasons.

? Why do you think all top clubs and star football players in the UK support the Kick It Out! campaign?

Young and Powerful

Young and Powerful is a group of young disabled and non-disabled people supported by Comic Relief. They all go to mainstream schools and campaign for **'inclusive education'**. They believe all children need to be taught together, so they can learn from each other.

? What does the phrase 'inclusive education' mean?

? What kinds of physical barriers would a wheelchair-user face if they came to your school? Would they face any other kinds of barriers?

Check your understanding

1 What is prejudice? Why are some people prejudiced against others?

2 What is discrimination? Give some examples.

3 Look at the different cases on these two pages and say whether the people or groups described could have experienced prejudice, discrimination or persecution.

4 How are the people in each story overcoming prejudice?

Discuss

1 In pairs, discuss how the following elements create barriers between individuals and groups:
- fear
- ignorance
- upbringing
- insecurity
- bad experiences.

Refer to the groups or individuals mentioned on these two pages to support your answers.

2 What kinds of barriers might people face as they get older (for example, when they retire)? How can young people help them to overcome these barriers?

Find out

Use the Kick It Out! website, **www.kickitout.org**, to research what your local football clubs, professional and amateur, are doing to combat racism.

Key terms

homophobic: fear or hatred of homosexuals

inclusive education: schooling that involves everyone, regardless of disability or non-disability

racism: the idea that some people of different origins are not as good as others

Discrimination and the law

Objective

Understand how the law works to protect people against discrimination.

Getting you thinking

WHO SAYS ETHNIC MINORITIES CAN'T GET JOBS? THERE ARE OPENINGS EVERYWHERE.

COMMISSION FOR RACIAL EQUALITY

1 What message is the poster giving?

2 What other forms of discrimination take place at work?

3 Why do people need protection against discrimination?

4 How do you think the law can help?

Fighting discrimination with the law

Everyone deserves a fair chance to be successful in life. Poster campaigns and other public awareness programmes try to educate people to think beyond prejudice. These campaigns are just one way of dealing with **discrimination**. There are also legal ways of tackling prejudice and discrimination. There are three important anti-discrimination laws:

The Sex Discrimination Act

Sex discrimination generally works against the interests of females, and particularly in the workplace. It can be difficult to ensure that women have the same opportunities for promotion as men when many have time away at some point to have children. However, although the Act usually protects women, if a man is unfairly treated because he is a man, he is also protected by the Act.

The Race Relations Act

The Race Relations Act makes it an offence to treat a person differently on grounds of race, colour, nationality, and national or ethnic origin. In practice, most racial discrimination in Britain is against people from ethnic minorities, but people from every nationality are protected by the law.

The Disability Discrimination Act

This Act aims to end discrimination against disabled people. A disability should not stop a person from being employed unless it stops them doing the job. Employers must help their staff. A deaf employee working in an office should be given a videophone to allow them to work like everybody else.

Look at these cases where the anti-discrimination Acts have helped people.

£60 000 for blind teacher

A blind teacher who became 'a burden' where she worked has received £60 000 in damages after an employment tribunal ruled that her school broke the law by failing to provide a classroom assistant to help her.

Liz Abbott, who was born with a visual impairment and is registered blind, won her case.

The Guardian, 5 July, 2000

? What explanation might the school give for not wanting to provide a classroom assistant? The court decided this reason was unfair. Explain why.

Ford's president signs pact to end Dagenham racism

Three years ago, the company apologized and paid **compensation** to four black workers after white faces were imposed on their photographs in a sales brochure. The following year, Ford had to pay out more than £70 000 compensation to seven Asian and Afro-Caribbean workers at Dagenham who were turned down for jobs in the truck fleet, where pay is roughly double the shop floor average but fewer than 2% of workers are from ethnic minorities, compared with 45% across the factory.

The Guardian, 26 October 1999

? Explain why the company had to pay compensation to the four black workers and the seven Asian and Afro-Caribbean workers.

? What does the figure of 2% of ethnic minorities working in the truck fleet compared with 45% in the rest of the factory suggest about discrimination at the factory at that time?

Single mother wins case over 16-hour shifts

A SINGLE mother, who was sacked for refusing to work 16-hour shifts at Heathrow, last night spoke of her relief after winning a sex discrimination case.

The Guardian, 3 August 1999

? Do you think the woman would have won the case if she wasn't a mother and she had refused to work the 16-hour shifts?

? Do you think a father would have been sacked if he had refused to work 16-hour shifts? What about a single father?

Find out

1 What does your school do to ensure equal opportunities for all students and staff?

2 Contact SCOPE or look on their website (**www.scope.org.uk**) and find out about their Schools Access Initiative.

Check your understanding

1 List the Acts which protect people from discrimination. Think of some situations when people might need to use these laws.

Key terms

compensation: making amends for something; something given to make good a loss

discrimination – racial, sex and disability: when a person is treated less favourably because of their colour, ethnic origins, gender or disability

What are human rights?

Getting you thinking

1 What are these children deprived of?

2 Make a list of the things you think every child should have.

3 Turn your list into a statement of children's rights.

Human rights

People all over the world suffer because their basic needs are not met. Some people's freedoms are limited by the country where they live. Nobody should live without these basic **human rights**:

- the right to education
- the right to work
- the right to fair conditions at work
- the right to travel
- the right to food and clothes
- the right to healthcare
- the right to meet with friends
- the right to own property
- to right to follow your religion
- the right to marry and have children
- the rights of minorities to be treated the same as the majority

? Which of the rights listed are the most important to you? Why?

? Can you think of some situations where any of your rights might be threatened?

? What examples are there in the news of people's human rights being threatened?

Human rights milestones

Ever since the end of World War II, people have been concerned about human rights. During the war, many people had been badly treated because of their race, religion or because they were prisoners of war.

The asylum seekers are escaping from Human Rights abuses

1948: Universal Declaration of Human Rights (UDHR)

The UDHR was drawn up by world leaders who wanted to prevent such terrible things happening again. It states that everyone has a right to life and liberty, freedom of speech and movement, a fair wage, a fair trial, education, and many other basic human rights.

1950: The European Convention on Human Rights (ECHR)

This sets the framework for European countries. If the residents of one country don't think they have had a fair response from the courts, they can take their case to the European Court of Human Rights.

Human Rights Act (UK)

The UK now has its own laws on human rights which say that all organizations have a duty to protect the rights of all individuals (as set out in the EHCR). The Human Rights **Act** protects everyone in the UK.

The case of A versus The United Kingdom

In 1993, a nine-year-old English boy, known as 'A', was beaten with a garden cane by his stepfather. When the stepfather was taken to court his defence was that English law says a parent can use 'reasonable force' to punish a child. He was found not guilty.

The boy's lawyers then took his case to the European Court of Human Rights, which decided the boy had suffered 'cruel, inhuman and degrading punishment'.

The boy was awarded £10000 in damages and the UK government agreed to change the law to give better protection to children in the future.

1981: The Convention on the Rights of the Child (CRC)

This **Convention** requires governments all around the world to think about the needs of young people, and to consult them about matters that affect them, such as education, family life, law and order.

Millions of young people do not have relatives to look after them – those caught up in civil wars in Africa, for instance. The CRC recognizes this and says that young people must have rights of their own – rights which don't depend on parents or other adults.

The CRC states: 'Governments should not allow children under 15 to join the army.'

Check your understanding

1 Why was the Universal Declaration of Human Rights written?

2 What is the main difference between the scope of the Universal Declaration of Human Rights and the European Convention on Human Rights?

3 What can European citizens do if they feel their human rights are being denied?

4 Why was the Convention on the Rights of the Child written?

Key terms

Act: a law passed by parliament

Convention: an agreement (often between governments)

Declaration: a document setting down aims and intentions

human rights: something people are morally or legally allowed to do or have

Action

Collect newspaper reports and internet articles concerned with human rights. Discuss the effects that being deprived of these rights can have on people.

Legal rights

Objective

Understand how the law is used to protect people's human rights.

Getting you thinking

1 What do the photographs tell you about human rights in USA in the mid-1900s?

2 Which basic human rights were being denied?

3 Do you think you would see sights like these in the USA today? Give reasons.

What are legal rights?

When law protects a human right, it becomes a **legal right**. For example, everyone has the right to go to public places such as parks, hotels and restaurants. The Race Relations Act makes it illegal for anyone to be refused entry to any public place because of his or her ethnicity. The Act also applies to employment and education. For example, it is illegal for an employer to tell someone, "You can't have the job because you're black." Similarly, it would be illegal to set up a school that accepted only black students.

The Race Relations Act is just one law among many that protects people's rights.

The Universal Declaration of Human Rights also says you have a right to 'equal pay for equal work'. The Sex Discrimination Act made equal pay a legal right.

The Universal Declaration of Human Rights says you have a right to a fair wage. In 1998 the Minimum Wage Act made this is a legal right, so all adult workers in England and Wales must be paid the minimum wage.

Legal rights and age limits

Everyone has basic rights. Some are limited by law.

Some of your legal rights in the UK

Drive a car
Vote in an election
Make a will
Pilot a plane

Criminal
responsibility

Buy a pet
on your own

10 12 14 16 18 20

Get a part-time job

Get married
Leave school
Work full time
Buy a lottery ticket
Ride a moped

? Why does the law impose age limits like the ones above?

? Which of these age limits would you change (raise or lower) and why?

? Whose human rights are being protected by each of these age limits?

Turning human rights into legal rights

★ the right to education
★ the right to work
★ the right to fair conditions at work
★ the right to travel
★ the right to food and clothes
★ the right to healthcare
★ the right to meet with friends
★ the right to own property
★ to right to follow your religion

★ the right to marry and have children
★ the rights of minorities to be treated the same as the majority
★ the right to life
★ the right to freedom
★ the right to privacy
★ the right to fair trial
★ the right not to be tortured or punished cruelly
★ the right to vote

? Can these human rights all be turned into legal rights? Give reasons.

? Suggest what these laws might say.

Legal rights are looked at throughout this book. You have already seen how there are laws protecting your right to follow your religion (pages 24–25) and how. The Race Relations Act and The Disability Discrimination Act (pages 30–31) help to protect the rights of minorities.

In the rest of the course you will learn about laws protecting rights at work (pages 40–43) and laws to do with privacy (pages 86–87).

Check your understanding

1 What is the difference between a human right and a legal right?

2 Name one law which makes a human right a legal right.

3 What does the phrase 'sex discrimination' mean? Give an example.

Find out

Research at what age and under what conditions young people have a legal right to drink alcohol. Carry out a survey to find out what your group thinks about these rights and age limits. How easy is it to police these laws?

Key terms

legal right: a right which is protected by law

Rights with responsibilities

Getting you thinking

In 1999, over 1000 people were injured by fireworks, and some seriously

Firework injuries (Oct–Nov 1999) in the UK

Age groups of those injured

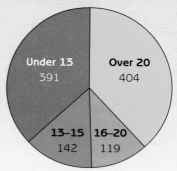

Under 13
391

Over 20
404

13–15
142

16–20
119

The place where people were injured

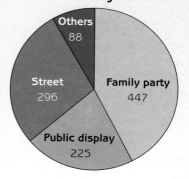

Others
88

Street
296

Family party
447

Public display
225

Total injuries 1056

RoSPA 2001

1 You must be over 18 to buy fireworks, and yet 50 per cent of all injuries were to children under 15. Are any of the following to blame for these accidents:

● companies which make fireworks
● shops which sell fireworks
● parents
● people who organize public displays
● the police
● the children themselves?

Give reasons.

2 What would you do to reduce the number of accidents with fireworks?

3 Turn your suggestions for question 2 into a firework safety code.

Rights and responsibilities

Everyone over 18 has a right to buy fireworks. This right, like many others, brings with it certain **responsibilities**. You must follow the firework code: never throw a lighted firework at anyone, and never set them off in the street where they might disturb elderly neighbours who have a right to peace and quiet, or alarm pets. The age limit for buying fireworks is set by law at 18 because this is the age at which the law expects people to be responsible enough to handle fireworks.

Rights and responsibilities are best thought of as two sides of the same coin. You have a right to own a bike and ride it down your street, but you also have a responsibility to ride it carefully so you don't endanger pedestrians or other road-users. For example, if you ride without lights in the dusk or dark you could cause a motorist to swerve and crash trying to avoid you. If this person needed their car to do their job, though no one was hurt in the accident, there will be financial consequences for the driver.

What responsibilities do these people have? What responsibilities do other people have towards them?

All children also have a right to an education – as expressed in the Convention of the Rights of the Child (CRC) – but students have a responsibility not to disrupt lessons so others can't learn.

You have a right to be **respected**, but you must also respect others. For example, you have a right to follow a particular religion and would expect your religious views to be respected. In the same way, you must respect the religious views of others.

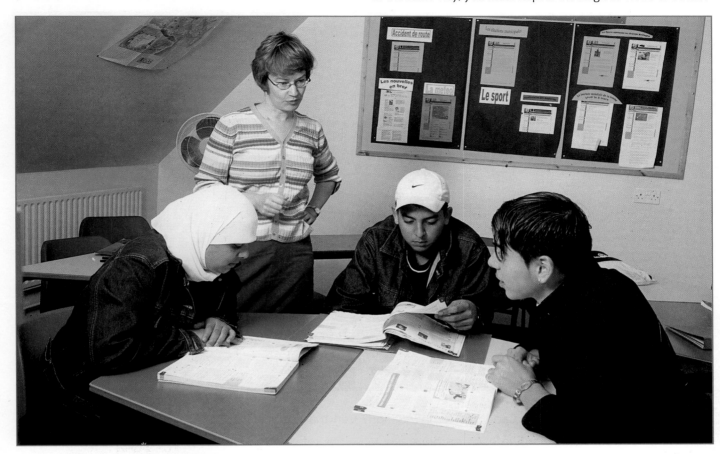

Needs and wants

What you have a *right* to and what you *want* are not the same thing. For instance, the Convention on the Rights of a Child states that you have the right to 'clean water and healthy food'. You might say: "I don't like drinking water. I want cola or coffee or champagne!" But the CRC focuses on the most *basic* human rights and needs, which are denied to millions of people all over the world and isn't about 'wants'.

As living standards rise and countries become richer, people's 'wants' increase too. Most UK families would say that televisions, washing machines, central heating and fridges are 'basic' household items, but our great-grandparents would have considered them luxuries.

Discuss

Suggest reasons why people in less economically developed countries (LEDCs) do not have their basic needs.

Key terms

respect: to have a good opinion of someone

responsibilities: something it is your duty to do or to look after

Check your understanding

1 List some responsibilities which go with the following rights:
  ● the right to an education
  ● the right to drink alcohol
  ● the right to own and drive a car.

2 Sort the following into two lists 'Wants' and 'Needs'.

healthy food	'A' levels
holidays	fashionable clothes
a good job	friends
healthcare	pocket money
TV in your room	
clean air	free travel to school
sex education	
parents/adults who look after you	

Now add five or six more items to each list.

Protecting the customer

Objective

Understand that there are laws to help consumers get a fair deal.

Getting you thinking

They said it would remove oil and grease but it doesn't. I followed the washing instructions, but the colours ran and stained my other clothes.

I bought a computer over the internet, but it doesn't work. The company I bought it from says I have signed my rights away.

These shoes just don't suit me. They looked good when I tried them on in the shop.

1 Match these questions to the situations.
Can I get my money back? Can I get compensation? Can that be true?

2 Who do you think is at fault in each of the examples – the retailer, manufacturer or **consumer**?

3 Are there any examples where the consumer is to blame?

What are my rights?

When you buy something from a shop, by mail order or through the internet, you are called a consumer and, as a consumer, you have certain rights. You are also a consumer when you pay someone to provide a service, such as a hairdresser, a photographer or an accountant.

Some of the most important laws protecting consumers' rights include:

- the **Trade Descriptions Act**, which makes it a criminal offence to make misleading price claims about goods or services. For example, "Was £200. Now £149.99" is misleading if the goods have never been sold at the higher price. If a film processor offers a one-hour service, this must be true.

- the **Sale and Supply of Goods Act**, which is concerned that goods sold must be of satisfactory quality and fit for the purpose they are sold and advertised for.

- the **Food Safety Act**, which covers the preparation and selling of food and drink in both shops and restaurants. The Act makes it an offence to sell or serve food or drink that is unsafe.

- the **Consumer Protection Act**, which means that consumers can claim for damages if they are injured as a result of using faulty goods. If a child was hurt by an unsafe toy, the manufacturers could be prosecuted.

Food safety officers have the power to inspect food that is being processed or that is for sale. Restaurants can be closed down if they serve unsafe food or drink.

How can you enforce your rights?

If you have bought goods or services and you are dissatisfied with them, you have a right to claim your money back, to an exchange or to a repeat of the service.

1 Contact the trader with details of your complaint, say what you want done and give them a chance to put the matter right.

2 If you are not happy with the outcome you can seek advice from the **Citizens Advice Bureau** (CAB). They can help with a wide variety of problems, including shopping complaints.

3 The Citizens Advice Bureau may recommend you go to a **Trading Standards Department**. They can investigate complaints about misleading descriptions or prices, and the safety of consumer goods. They can take action against people who break the law.

4 The **Office of Fair Trading** – a government office – can also take action against traders who break consumer laws.

A Trading Standards Officer inspecting dangerous baby equipment

Home shopping and the internet

When you buy over the internet (from a company trading in the UK), you are covered by more or less the same legislation as those that cover shop purchases:

- the goods you've bought should be of satisfactory quality
- fit for the purpose they are sold for
- as described by the seller.

Sellers have rights too

Consumers cannot claim refunds or demand exchanges in certain situations. If you bought a shirt in a sale and you knew it had a defect, you would not be able to claim your money back because the seller didn't hide the problem from you when you bought it.

Sellers do not have to exchange goods, but most will do so as long as they have not been used. So, if you have bought some clothes and you change your mind about them later, you will find most shops are happy to exchange them – even though they don't have to by law.

Check your understanding

1 If you bought a CD at a reduced price because the CD cover was damaged, would you be able to take it back to the shop and claim a refund? Give reasons for your answer.

2 If you bought something from a shop and it was faulty but the shop refused to refund your money, what could you do?

3 What extra rights do you have when home shopping or shopping over the internet, compared with when you buy something from a shop?

Discuss

1 In pairs, think about why traders and businesses prefer to sort out complaints themselves.

2 Do you think it is important to have consumer rights? Give reasons. What could happen if they didn't exist?

Key terms

Citizens Advice Bureau (CAB): an organization that offers free advice on consumer and other legal matters

consumer: a person who buys goods or services for their own needs

Trading Standards Department: an official body that enforces consumer-based laws

Fair play at work

Getting you thinking

Many people work on computers all day. Their employers may have set them tough targets to meet.

1. What sorts of problems do you think people might face when at work?

2. How do you think an employer might make people's working lives better?

3. What effect do you think a happy workforce has on a business?

4. What do you think the law should have to say about working conditions?

Why do we need employment laws?

Employment laws exist to protect employees and make sure businesses carry out their responsibilities towards their staff. Without these laws people's human right to fair conditions at work could be harder to protect.

Exploiting people

Before laws were introduced to protect people, some employers treated their staff unfairly. Employees suffered though:

- long hours
- dangerous and unhealthy working conditions
- poor pay
- not being treated as individuals, with individual needs.

There was no government support in terms of unemployment benefit or sickness pay, so employees could not afford to argue with their employers, nor could they afford to be ill.

Unions

Employees began to form **trade unions**. They negotiated with employers to reach fairer agreements on pay and working conditions. Over the years these agreements led to huge improvements in the rights of employees.

By trying to persuade employers and Parliament to adopt fairer and safer working practices, the Unions proved to be an effective **pressure group** in looking after the interests of their members. A group of people bargaining together is more powerful than individuals working alone.

Unions helped to form the Labour Party

How does the law protect?

The **Contract of Employment** is an agreement between employer and employee setting out the pay and conditions, including holiday entitlements.

The **Equal Pay Act** means that men and women in jobs which require the same effort, skills or responsibility should be paid the same amount.

The **Sex Discrimination Act** and the **Race Relations Act** protect individuals from being treated differently because of their sex, nationality or ethnicity.

Health and safety laws are designed to reduce accidents. Employers must provide a safe working environment and train employees to work safely.

European regulations

Some European Union members have signed up to a Social Chapter. The Chapter sets employment rights, such as maternity and paternity leave, so everyone has guaranteed working conditions.

The UK has not signed the Chapter because higher wages and better conditions would push up the business costs. UK businesses would therefore become less competitive in other countries where rules are not so strict.

Check your understanding

1 Who do unions represent and what are they trying to do?

2 What areas do the main employment laws cover?

Find out

Find out what unions provide for their members. Produce a union recruitment poster giving reasons why employees should join. You can get ideas from **www.tuc.org.uk** or **www.unison.org.uk**.

Key terms

employment laws: laws passed by Parliament and the European Union that set out the rights and responsibilities of employers and employees

pressure group: a group of people who try to change public opinion or government policy to their own views or beliefs

trade unions: organizations that look after the interests of a group of employees

Responsibilities in the workplace

Objective

Understand that both employers and employees have responsibilities in the workplace.

Getting you thinking

What Asda expects from you

Attendance

If you don't come to work, your work has to be done by your colleagues and it reduces our opportunity to offer good customer service. However, sometimes absence from work is unavoidable. If you can't come to work, please contact the store no later than two hours before the start of your shift.

Punctuality

Customers expect us to be available to give them the service they want, so all colleagues must avoid lateness.

Appearance

Colleagues must wear the uniform provided by the Company and adhere to the dress standards.

Friends and relatives

Colleagues must not serve relatives or friends at either counters or checkouts.

Mobile phones

Colleagues are allowed to make personal calls during their break times from pay phones provided in store. Colleagues may not carry or use personal mobile phones whilst working.

1 Explain each of ASDA's rules.

2 Why does ASDA expect its staff have a responsible attitude to their work?

3 ASDA expects it staff to be responsible. What should the staff expect from ASDA?

Your responsibilities as an employee

Just as employers have responsibilities towards their employees, so the employees have responsibilities towards their employer.

Employees must carry out their responsibilities as set out in the **contract of employment**. Employees should receive this within eight weeks of starting a new job. This contract sets out what the employer and the employee are expected to do. This is important – there are two sides to the contract and both the employer and employee must do what they have agreed to. If the employee fails to do this, they can be dismissed. If the employer doesn't keep their side of the contract, the employee can take them to an **employment tribunal**.

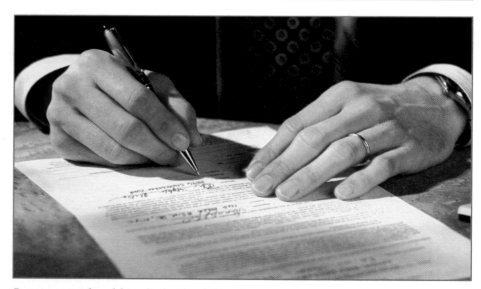

A contract should include the following:

- names of employer and employee
- date of starting
- rate of pay and working hours
- place of work
- holiday entitlement
- entitlement to sick pay
- pension details (if any)
- complaints and disciplinary procedures
- conditions for ending the employment contract.

Check your understanding

1 What is the contract of employment for?

2 What reasons can be given for dismissal?

3 What is the difference between dismissal and redundancy?

4 What can an employee do if they feel they have been treated unfairly?

Find out

Look in a local or national paper to see if there are any reports of an industrial tribunal. What was the issue? Who won? Why? Had one side acted irresponsibly? If so, explain how.

Key terms

contract of employment: a document which details an employee's, and employer's responsibilities for a particular job

dismissal: when employers end an employee's contract of employment (sometimes called 'sacking')

employment tribunal: a type of court dealing only with disagreements over employment laws

redundancy: when a person loses their job because the job doesn't need to be done anymore

warning: written or spoken warnings given by an employer to an employee if the employer thinks the employee has been breaking the contract of employment

People can be dismissed if they are unable to do the job properly or have been involved in any misconduct, such as fighting, discrimination, deliberate damage or theft. A minor misconduct, such as bad time keeping, usually results in verbal **warning**. If this continues it will become a written warning and with no further improvement can end in **dismissal**. A major misconduct, like theft, can lead to instant dismissal.

Dismissal is different from **redundancy**. Redundancy occurs when the job has ended and no one is being taken on to replace you. It is the employer's responsibility and the employee will receive a payment at least equivalent to one month's pay for every year employed by the business.

What if it all goes wrong?

There might be a disagreement between the employer and the employee over a dismissal. If it can't be sorted out the case can be taken to an employment tribunal. This is a type of court of law that has the power to fine the business and make it pay damages to the employee if it finds that the employee was not to blame. If the dismissed person belongs to a union they can seek advice from it and the union can represent them at the tribunal. Sometimes tribunals come out in favour of the employer and sometimes in favour of the employee.

What's the point of law?

Getting you thinking

1 This group of friends all live together. They left home a year ago and rent a house together. Two of them work during the day, one sometimes works a night shift and two are students. What kinds of things do they have to think about and remember to do because they live together? Might there be any situations that could lead to disagreements between them?

2 Imagine you are in a similar situation. Which rules would you make to ensure that the house ran as smoothly as possible?

Why do people obey the law?

Law-abiding citizens will obey the law for a variety of reasons: they may be afraid of being caught and arrested; it may be the shame that going to prison would bring on them and their family; they don't want their 'good name' (their reputation) damaged; or they may have strong religious or moral views about breaking the law.

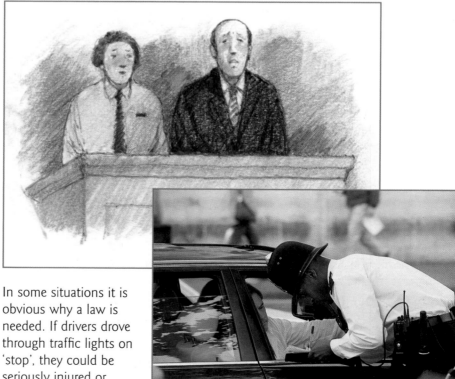

In some situations it is obvious why a law is needed. If drivers drove through traffic lights on 'stop', they could be seriously injured or killed, or cause injury or death to someone else.

Why don't people obey the law?

A shoplifter, who has stolen a couple of T-shirts, might argue that it won't put a big company like Marks and Spencer out of business. But:

- if everybody stole from them it would push up prices for everyone else who shops there because Marks and Spencer had to pay for the T-shirts

- if you steal from Marks and Spencer, you steal from the people who own the business, so it's just like stealing a mobile phone or a car.

In the same way, if people don't pay income tax when they should, the government will have less money to pay for schools and hospitals; so many people are affected *indirectly* by tax evasion.

Why do laws change?

There are laws to cover a vast range of activities, including adoption, marriage and divorce, terrorism, **discrimination**, motoring, banking, sex, drugs, theft and assault. New developments, such as cloning or the internet, often require new laws.

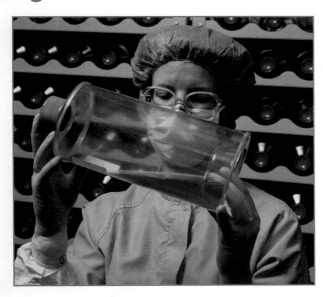

Why do we need laws?

The short answer is, try imagining life without them! Your life would be chaotic, and the most vulnerable members of society, such as the very young, the elderly, the ill, and some minorities, would suffer most. What would happen to children, for example, if there were no laws on divorce?

For laws to work properly they need the support of the majority of the population. Most people agree that child abuse is a shocking crime and abusers must be punished. But public opinion is more divided on euthanasia. Some think it wrong to treat doctors as criminals if they help terminally ill patients in pain to die. Others would argue that this is morally wrong as well as unlawful.

Find out

Research some laws that are currently going through parliament. As a class, choose three laws and write to your MP to ask which of these laws they support and why.

Discuss

1 In groups, think about your usual daily routine and list how many times during the day you come across a rule or law. Why do you choose to obey or not to obey these rules and laws?

2 You sometimes hear people say "But it's a bad law." Make a list of your reasons for laws being good or bad. Be ready to explain your ideas.

Check your understanding

1 In your own words, give four reasons why people obey the law. Suggest one more reason not mentioned on these pages.

2 Make a list of crimes that have immediate consequences for the general public. List others that may have long-term and then less immediate consequences.

3 Why do you think it is important that the majority of citizens support a particular law? Suggest one law that probably has majority support. Suggest one that probably doesn't, and give a reason.

Civil and criminal law – what's the difference?

Getting you thinking

Neighbours go to court over right to access land

Police raid drug den

1 Which case is a private issue?

2 Which case is more likely to have the police involved? Give reasons.

3 Which case is more worrying for the general public? Why?

Two kinds of law

Over many centuries of law making, two separate but related branches of the law have evolved to meet changing circumstances: civil law and criminal law.

Most civil cases are about disputes between individuals or groups, and very often these arguments are about rights. Examples include company law, adoption, accidents at work and consumer rights.

Criminal law deals with offences such as murder, theft and drug dealing. In a criminal case, the conflict is between the government (acting for all citizens) and the lawbreakers.

Who's right?

The person who brings a case to a civil court is called the claimant. The person accused of doing wrong is called the defendant. In some civil cases, the claimant sets out to sue the defendant. If the claimant wins, the defendant will have to give them money.

*July 2001: England football coach, Sven-Goran Eriksson, **sues** Hello! magazine. He says the magazine invaded his privacy and published photographs of his home without his permission.*

? Who is the claimant in the Sven-Goran Eriksson case? Who is the defendant?

? Why will this case be heard in a civil court?

What happens in a civil court?

Most civil cases are heard in a **county court**. Because a court case can be very expensive, most people try to settle the dispute before it gets to court.

A small number of civil cases are heard in a **High Court**. These courts deals with complex family disputes and other complicated financial and legal matters, such as bankruptcy and large claims for damages. Any case involving £50 000 or more is heard in the High Court.

If a civil case involves a claim of less than £5 000 it will be heard in a **small claims court**. About 90 000 cases a year are heard in these courts.

A civil court
*A **judge** sitting without a **jury** decides almost all civil cases.*

Criminal courts
*There is a separate system of courts to deal with criminal cases. Less serious offences are dealt with in **magistrates' courts**. Serious offences are dealt with in **crown courts** before a judge and a jury.*

Find out

Make a list of the different types of cases heard in a civil court. Pick one of these and say what human rights might be involved in such a case.

Action

Many civil cases are the result of disputes between neighbours. Discuss what makes a good neighbour. Produce a 'Good Neighbours Charter' – some common sense rules to help neighbours to avoid disputes.

Check your understanding

1 What are the main differences between civil and criminal cases?

2 What is (a) a claimant, (b) a defendant and (c) a small claims court?

3 What type of crime is dealt with in either the magistrates' or crown courts?

Key terms

civil law: this covers disputes between individuals or groups. Civil law cases are often about rights

county court: a local court that has limited powers in civil cases (laws operating between people)

criminal law: this deals with offences such as murder and drug dealing. These cases are between the Crown Prosecution Service (acting for all citizens) and the offender

crown court: courts held in towns in England and Wales where judges hear cases

High Court: the court where judges hear cases on serious crimes

judge: a person who decides questions of law in a court

jury: a group of people who decide if someone is guilty in a court of law

magistrates' court: a court held before two or more public officers dealing with minor crimes

small claims court: a local court, which hears civil cases involving small amounts of money

sue: to make a claim against someone or something

Who puts the law into practice?

Objective

Understand the various roles of people who work within the criminal justice system.

Getting you thinking

1 You've broken the law and have to appear in court. Which of the following would you prefer as your 'judge and jury', and why:

- your teachers
- your classmates
- your parents
- the police
- other young people who've been in trouble themselves
- the victims of your crime
- a group of people chosen at random, who do not know you?

2 Which group do you think the victim would prefer? Give reasons.

3 Which group do you think would give the fairest outcome? Give reasons.

The criminal justice system

The criminal justice system is large and complex. These are the roles within it.

Judges

The judges that work in both criminal and civil courts are known collectively as the **judiciary**. Most judges have worked for at least 10 years as a barrister, but a few solicitors also become judges. In a jury trial, it is the jury who decide if the accused is guilty or not, but the judge who determines the sentence.

Senior judges (who sit in the higher courts) are very powerful. They don't make laws – Parliament does that – but if there is an argument about how a law should be interpreted, it is senior judges who decide.

Magistrates

Full-time magistrates

Full-time (paid) magistrates are called district judges. They are usually barristers or solicitors with at least seven years' experience. They sit alone.

Part-time magistrates

Part-time magistrates come from all walks of life. They are not legally qualified and are not paid. They work with other magistrates.

Jury

A jury is made up of 12 adults, who sit in a crown court and decide whether the accused is innocent or guilty. A jury is made up of members of the public chosen at random.

Police

The police do not make laws – they enforce them. Their job is to protect the public, arrest lawbreakers and bring them before the courts.

Solicitors

All solicitors must pass law exams because, among other things, they can give legal advice to people who have to go to court. Some solicitors also speak in court on behalf of their their clients.

Barristers

Barristers undergo a long legal training too, but they spend most of their time in court representing their clients. They are the only lawyers qualified to speak in any type of court.

Probation officers

If an offender is given a community sentence (see page 53), they will work with a local probation officer. Probation officers are professionally qualified. They write court reports on offenders and supervise them in the community when they've been sentenced.

Discuss

1. What skills and personal qualities do you think you need to be a good magistrate?

2. Can you think of any reasons why people don't apply to be magistrates?

3. List some reasons why being a police office can be a rewarding but stressful job.

4. Why are relations between police and young people sometimes poor?

Find out

1. Research the entry requirements (that is, age, qualifications, etc.) of either a police officer or a solicitor.

2. Interview a probation officer to find out about the work they do with offenders in the community. You may wish to research a specific aspect of their work. For example, probation officers often work with young offenders who have problems with alcohol and other drugs.

3. Research who can be called for jury service and what serving on a jury involves.

Check your understanding

1. What do judges do in trials where there is a jury?

2. What powers do senior judges have?

3. What is the most important difference between the role of the police and the role of judges?

4. What is the difference between a barrister and a solicitor?

Key terms

judiciary: all the judges in a country

Criminal courts

Objective

Understand the difference between a magistrates' court and a crown court.

Getting you thinking

1 Which of the two courtrooms above is the most 'child-friendly' and why?

2 Should courts be made more 'adult-friendly'? Give reasons.

3 Is it good idea that courts are open to the public? Give reasons.

Courts are formal places. Everyone involved must take the process very seriously. In some countries, youth courts are more informal because people think young people are more likely to tell the truth in a more relaxed environment.

There are two types of court for criminal cases – magistrates' courts and crown courts.

Who's who in a magistrates' court?

Over 95 per cent of all criminal trials take place in magistrates' courts. Specially-trained **magistrates** also run youth courts for offenders aged between 10 and 17. Magistrates, who sit in court with at least one other magistrate, also deal with a small number of civil cases and grant licences to pubs, clubs and betting shops.

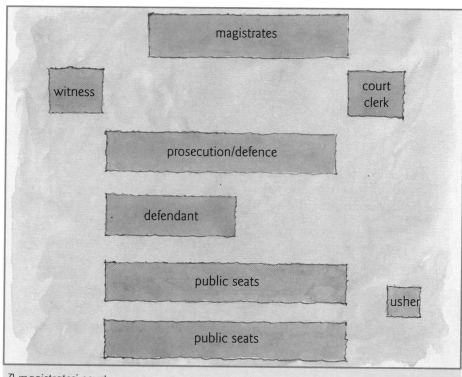

A magistrates' court

50

Mitigating factors

There is no jury in a magistrates' court, so magistrates must be absolutely sure 'beyond reasonable doubt' that the accused is guilty. They must also take into account any **mitigating** factors. If, for example, a woman stole from a supermarket because she had no money to buy food for herself and her children, magistrates would take this into account and may give her a lesser sentence.

What sentences can magistrates give?

Magistrates have the power to give the following penalties:

- prison – up to a maximum of six months
- community sentences*
- fines – up to a maximum £5000
- discharge – conditional or absolute*.

(*see page 53)

A crown court

The most serious criminal cases are heard in a crown court. The atmosphere is more solemn and the proceedings more formal than in a magistrates' court. The judges and barristers wear wigs and gowns. A jury decides if the defendant is guilty or not, unless the defendant pleads guilty – in which case no jury is involved.

Crown court judges can have different powers. Only High Court judges, who sit in the larger courts, can try very serious cases, such as murder and rape. Others – known as circuit judges and **recorders** – try less serious cases, such as theft.

Crown court judges and juries must also take into account any mitigating factors, in the same way that magistrates must. The maximum sentence in a crown court is life imprisonment.

Check your understanding

1 What are 'mitigating factors'? Support your answer with an example.

2 What kinds of mitigating factors might influence magistrates' decisions when sentencing young offenders?

3 List the differences between a magistrates' court and crown court.

4 What is the maximum sentence each type of court can impose?

5 When is a jury used in a crown court case?

Key terms

magistrate: a public officer who deals with civil cases

mitigating: making something less intense or severe

recorder: a barrister of solicitor of at least 10 years experience who acts as a part-time judge in a crown court

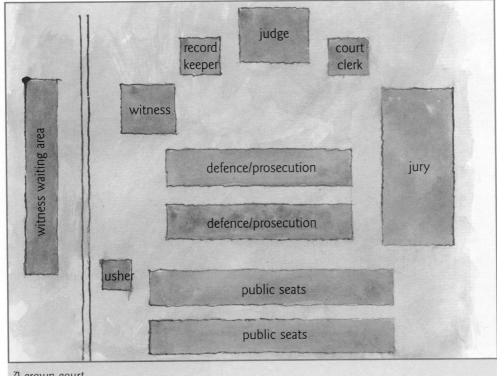

A crown court

What sentence?

Objective

Understand how magistrates and judges fit the sentence to the crime.

Getting you thinking

Mrs B: Stole £5000

Mr G: Stole £50

- Both Mrs B and Mr G should get the same sentence.
- Mrs B should get a tougher sentence because she stole more.
- Mrs B should get a lighter sentence because she is old and poor.
- Mrs B should get a lighter sentence because she's a woman.

1 Which would be the fairest decision? Give reasons.

Making the punishment fit the crime.

There is a range of sentences available to magistrates and judges. Sentences must follow guidelines laid down by the government, but these do allow some flexibility. It would be undesirable to have only one sentence for theft, for instance, as this might result in someone who stole £10 receiving the same punishment as someone who stole £10000.

What's the point of punishment?

Punishment Separation from friends and family, and the 'outside world'.

Public protection Did victims and others feel safer when they were locked up?

Deterrence Will the punishment stop them re-offending? Will it stop others offending?

Rehabilitation Have they learned any useful skills while they were inside? Have they learned to cope with their anger? Their drugs problem?

Disapproval Do they feel ashamed? Do they understand how law-abiding people feel about their crime?

? Which of the five reasons for punishing offenders do you think is the most important, and why? Which is the least?

Prison

You will be sent to prison if you commit a serious crime (for example, armed robbery), but only if you are over 21. Young offenders (18–21) are sent to a Young Offenders Institution.

Community sentences

If you are given a **community sentence** you don't go to prison. You will work with a probation officer in the community. If a community service order is imposed, you will work a set number of hours (usually at the weekend) cleaning up graffiti and litter, tidying gardens or building playgrounds.

If a curfew order is also imposed, you must be at home for up to 12 hours each day and electronic tags may be used to check on your whereabouts. If you have a problem with alcohol or other drugs, you may have to undergo regular drug tests and attend drug treatment classes.

An exclusion order prohibits you from going to pubs, football grounds and other places where you've previously caused trouble.

A reparation order means you do work for your victims (if they agree) to make up for any harm you did, financial or emotional.

Manchester United star Eric Cantona was sentenced to 120 hours community service after attacking a fan. He spent some of his sentence coaching young people.

Fines

Crown courts can impose unlimited fines, but the maximum fine in a magistrates' court is £5000. Any fine must reflect the offender's ability to pay. The maximum fine for 14- to 17-year-olds is £1000.

Discharge

If you are a first-time offender who has committed a minor offence, having to go to court is seen as punishment enough and you will probably get an absolute discharge. If you are given a conditional discharge you will have to keep out of trouble for a set period or you will be punished for the original offence.

Appeals

If you are found guilty but you do not think you had a fair trial, or you think the sentence is too harsh, you can in certain circumstances **appeal** against the sentence.

If you were found guilty in a magistrates' court, your appeal would usually be heard in a crown court.

Everyone has the right to appeal, but an appeal will only go ahead if you have a good reason. For instance, if your case had a lot of press coverage, this may have influenced the jury. If someone is convicted and their sentence seems light, the prosecutor can appeal too.

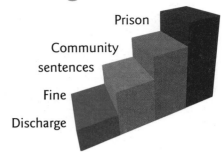

The range of sentences

Prison
Community sentences
Fine
Discharge

Check your understanding

1 When might a magistrate impose an exclusion order?

2 What is the difference between an absolute and a conditional discharge?

3 What are the two main reasons for appealing against a sentence?

Find out

Research ways in which community service orders are used with young offenders in your area. Are they 'a soft option'?

Discuss

In what ways does an offender's punishment sometimes continue after he or she has served their sentence?

Key terms

appeal: a request for a decision made by a court to reviewed

community sentence: when someone who has been convicted of a crime works in the community (clearing litter, for example) rather than going to prison

rehabilitation: restoring a person to normal life

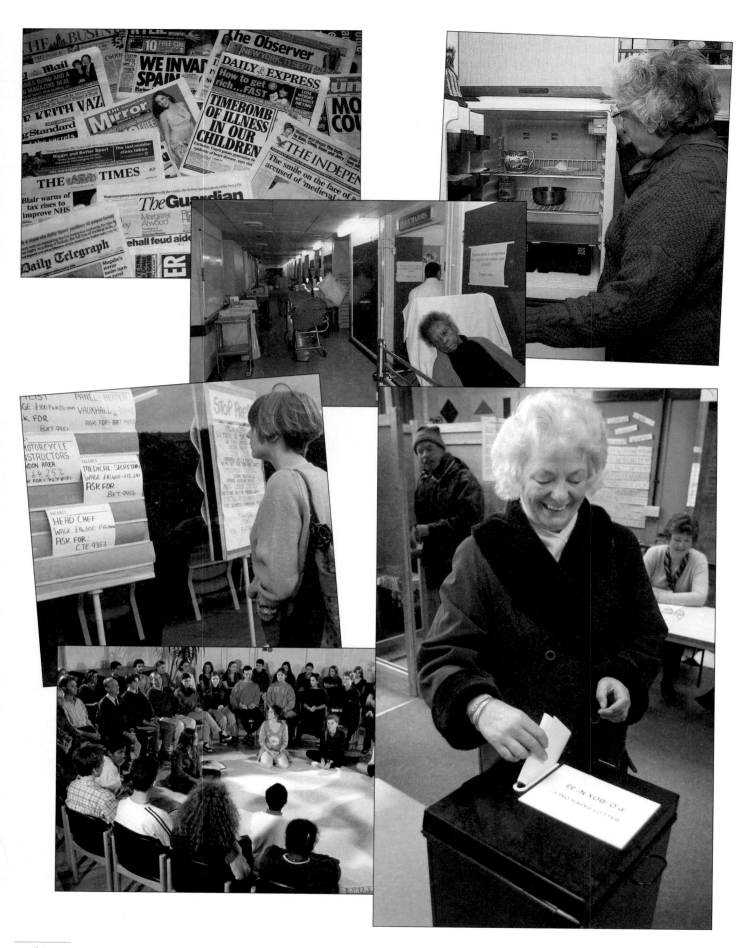

Theme 2 Power, politics and the media

Working together

Objective

Understand how and why people participate in the life of the school.

Getting you thinking

1 Make a list of the different ways in which students can take part in the life of this school.

2 How many other ways can you participate at your school?

3 Do you think it is important to have a wide range of ways that students can participate? Give reasons.

4 Do you think taking part in school activities affects how students think about the school?

School council

The school council will meet at 3.30 p.m. on 1 February in room SL13. Please make sure that all year groups have discussed the issues on the agenda with their representatives so that decisions can be taken at the meeting.

If there are other issues you want to raise, please discuss them in form time before the meeting.

Y10 community service teams

Briefing will take place at 1.20 p.m. next Tuesday. Please be sure to have told Mr Jones which task team you want to be in.

New headteacher

Interviews for the new headteacher take place next week. They will be viewing the school on Tuesday morning. The student interview panel should please report to the school office at 2 p.m. on Tuesday afternoon.

School football team comes top of the league again!

Congratulations to all those who have taken part. The season is not yet over but no one can overtake us now. The last three games might make it a year to remember!

Ski trip

Anyone in Years 9, 10 or 11 who is interested in joining the ski trip to Italy next year, please come to a meeting in room SR6 on Wednesday 7 February.

Concert rehearsals

The dress rehearsal for the concert is taking place on Thursday. Please turn up on time for your item. There are over 100 people involved so timing is important.

Joining in

All schools have different ways in which students can join in. For example, there are stories of students painting the social areas of their school or making an environmental garden, and many schools run projects where students work together to combat problems like bullying.

All these ways of joining in help people to have more respect for the school and their fellow students. If you have created and looked after something, or have worked hard to make the school a better place, you want it to stay like that. If you see others spoiling it in some way, you will probably want to stop them.

A school where there is lots of participation is likely to have many students who have a sense of belonging and, therefore, respect its way of life.

Students and staff during a school council meeting

Having a voice

There are other activities that help to run the school. Do you have a **school council**? In most cases where they operate, every class and year group has a representative on the school council. Sometimes there may be year-group councils because younger students can find it hard to be heard when in meetings with older students. The school council will discuss things that they want changing, or comment on proposals from the staff. When all students in school feel that they have a voice, they are likely to be happier about the decisions that are made.

The level of involvement of the council can vary, but many are consulted when important decisions, such as teacher appointments, are made. One newly appointed deputy headteacher said, "The toughest part of the whole interview was the one with the students." It was tough because he respected the students' views and knew that these were the people he had to be able to influence if he was to have a successful future. It's much easier to work with people if they respect you.

Choosing the representatives

When classes have to choose a member of the school council, they usually do it by holding an **election**. Students can either volunteer to stand, or they might be put forward by their friends. They are often asked to make a speech about their views, after which an election is held. In the election, everyone in the class can vote for the person who they want to be the class representative. The one with the most votes will join the school council. This representative will be responsible for listening to their classmates' opinions and standing up for these views in school council meetings. There are too many students in every school to make it easy for every individual opinion to be heard, so having one person to represent a group is a practical system.

This process of choosing and electing representatives is known as **representative democracy** – where people have a chance to vote for someone who they think will represent them. This happens in schools all over the country, but it also happens in elections in your local area and the whole country.

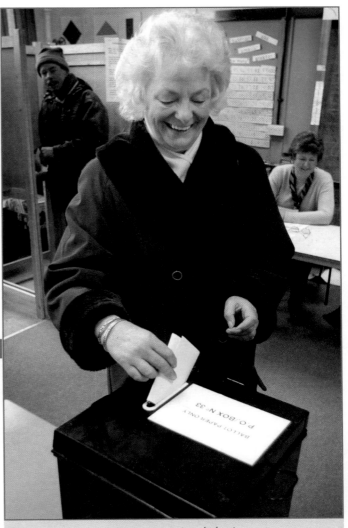
Choosing a representative in a national election

Find out

Does your school have a school council? If it does, what has it discussed recently? If it doesn't have a council, do you think it should? Why?

Discuss

1 What sorts of issues should be discussed by the school council?

2 "It's easier to work with people if they respect you." Do you agree with this statement? Give reasons. Think of examples where working together could be made easier if those taking part have more respect for each other.

Key terms

election: selection of one or more people for an official position by voting (in the UK, almost everyone over 18 can vote)

representative democracy: a type of democracy, where citizens have the right to choose someone to represent them on a council or in government

school council: a group of people who represent the classes and year groups of the school. They give students the opportunity to participate in decision making

Check your understanding

1 In your own words, say why it can be useful to have a school council.

2 What does 'representative democracy' mean?

Power, politics and the media

Who represents us?

Getting you thinking

Don't close the skate park!

Joe had just saved up enough to buy some in-line skates. He'd mastered going forwards and backwards, and was about to try out some new moves at the public skate park.

When he arrived, no one was skating. He found a group of people talking in one corner, all sounding very angry. They were looking at a notice pinned to the wall that read: THE SKATE PARK WILL CLOSE ON 31 OCTOBER.

Everyone was asking questions: "Why?" "Who decided?" "What about us?" "What can we do about it?" When they began to calm down, they made a plan. Joe suggested that they should complain to the local **council**. The council had become involved when there was trouble over parking outside his school so perhaps they could help now. Some of the people he talked to didn't know anything about the council. Joe explained that the council was made up of people who were chosen to represent different parts of the town. They all agreed to find out who represented them in their local areas – and to complain.

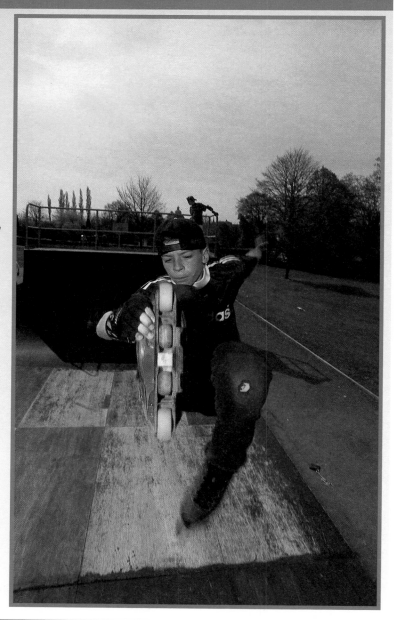

1 The skate park is for the use of local people. Who do you think should make decisions about it?

2 It is difficult for everyone in the area to be involved in every decision. How could it be made simpler?

3 What kinds of things should people make decisions about in their local area?

Representing everyone

Joe and his friends had an issue that they wanted to discuss – someone in the town had made a decision that they did not like. They wanted to find out who it was and why they had made it. Joe was right when he said they should talk to people on the council as, in this case, they would have been responsible for the decision.

The local council is made up of local people who make decisions about local services. These **councillors** represent different parts of the town, called **wards**. They are chosen in an election by the people who live in the ward.

WARMINGTON COUNCIL ELECTION

PUT ONE CROSS AGAINST
OF YOUR CHOIC

NAME	DES
1 ANNA McCLOUD	
2 HARI PATEL	
3 MAY GILBERT	
4 PETER MARRIOT	

In many areas elections take place every four years. **Political parties** put up candidates for people to choose between. Each party will have decided on a list of plans, called a **manifesto**, which it will put into practice if it wins enough seats on the council. Sometimes there is a long list of people to choose from at an election. Some will represent the well-known political parties like Labour, Conservative and the Liberal Democrats. Others will represent smaller groups like the Greens, or people who are campaigning on a local issue. Most councils are a mix of political parties, but the one with most councillors takes overall control.

Almost everyone who is aged 18 or more can vote in these elections. Just like the school council, the process is democratic because everyone can take part. Each year a form is sent to every house in the area to check who is entitled to vote.

Your vote is always secret, so nobody can check on your decision. Has your school or village hall been used as a **polling station** on election day?

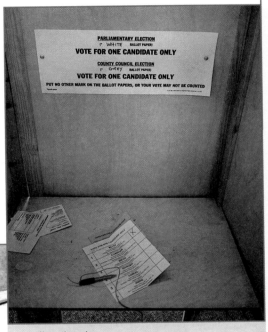

A polling booth

Find out

1 Find out who represents your area on the local council.

2 What is the mix of political parties that makes up your local council? Which one has overall control?

3 Find out about an issue that the council is discussing at the moment. What are the different points of view? Follow it up and find out what happens in the end.

Check your understanding

1 Who is on the local council?

2 How were these representatives chosen?

3 Why are most councils a mix of political parties?

Discuss

1 Why do you think it is important that your vote is secret?

2 Why do you think people want to become local councillors?

Key terms

council: a group of people who are elected to look after the affairs of a town, district or county

councillor: a member of a local council, elected by people in that area

manifesto: a published statement of the aims and policies of a political party

political party: organized groups of people with common aims who put up candidates up for elections

polling station: a place where votes are cast – often a school, library or village hall

ward: an area that forms a separate part of a local council

How does the council work?

Getting you thinking

Don't close the skate park II

Joe set about finding out how to contact the people at the council who could help with the skate park closure. He rang the main council switchboard and asked to talk to someone who could help him.

He was put through to the Leisure and Recreation department, who said that the council had made the decision because they wanted to use the money to provide better services for the elderly. There had also been some complaints from the neighbours next to the skate park because of the noise, and they were worried about what was going on. Joe was told to contact the member of the council's cabinet responsible for leisure. An email or letter might be the best way to make contact because being a councillor is a spare time job so they are at work during the day.

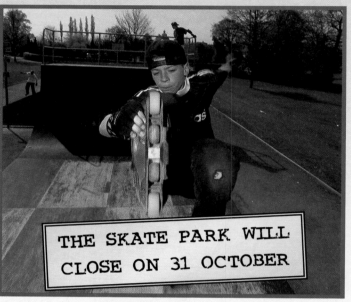

THE SKATE PARK WILL CLOSE ON 31 OCTOBER

1 Who makes decisions about local leisure and recreation issues?

2 What differences are there between the councillor and the person who works in the Leisure and Recreation department?

3 Why do you think the council has to make choices between spending money on the skate park and services for the elderly?

4 Why do you think the council takes notice of the people who complain about what goes on at the skate park?

How is the council organized?

Every area of the country elects a councillor. When the council first meets after an election, it elects a leader and the members of the **cabinet**. The leader and cabinet all come from the political party that won the most of votes – they have the **majority**.

Each member of the cabinet will have responsibility for one area of the council's work – for example, education, social services, finance, and leisure and recreation.

Apart from electing the cabinet, the council also elects Overview and Scrutiny committees to make sure the council is run properly.

Being a councillor carries a lot of responsibility, but the role is mainly voluntary. Councillors are paid travel expenses and an attendance fee for meetings, but they don't receive a salary.

How does the council do its work?

All the councillors meet to put together the plan for the year. They set the budget for each area of spending. The Overview and Scrutiny committees then make sure this plan is followed.

There are some areas, like planning for things like housing and road building, which the council as a whole controls. Planning decisions are made according to laws laid down by central government so the council sets up a committee to make sure that the rules are followed.

All councillors, whether they are members of the cabinet or not, must represent their ward in council decisions. They have a vote in council meetings and must use it in a way that serves their ward best.

As most of the people on the council have full-time jobs, they cannot run the services as well. A **Chief Executive** is appointed to take responsibility for this. In each department, people who are experts in their field are employed to make sure it all runs smoothly.

The structure of the council

The structure shown here is the one that is used most frequently around the UK.

Members of the political party which won the most seats at the election

Members of the other political parties and groups. Each member is responsible for one area of the local council's work

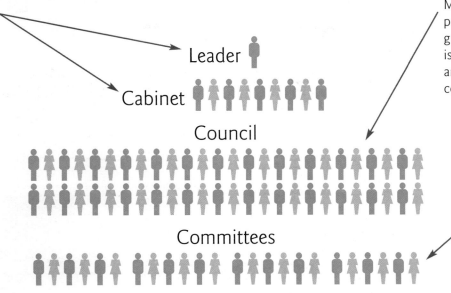

Leader

Cabinet

Council

Committees

These people make sure that the council sticks to its plan and budget for each year

Find out

Have a look at your local council's website. Two example addresses are:
www.suffolkcc.gov.uk
www.hullcc.gov.uk.

1 How is your council organized? Is there a cabinet and leader?

2 Which political party, if any, has control of your local council?

3 Find out about the work a councillor from your ward does.

4 Who would Joe have to talk to if his skate park was in your area?

Check your understanding

1 What does the council's cabinet do?

2 Who decides how much money to spend on each part of the council's work?

3 What do councillors do for their wards?

4 What's the difference between a councillor and a Chief Executive?

What is a mayor?

In most places, a **mayor** holds a ceremonial role. When the Queen or other famous people come to visit, the Mayor puts on the chain of office and meets them. However, in May 2002 elections for directly elected mayors were held in a number of towns for the first time.

Key terms

cabinet: the main decision-making body of the council

Chief Executive: an employee of the council, responsible for the smooth running of services

majority: the party with a majority has won a bigger proportion of the votes than the others

mayor: a member of the council who is selected to be its representative on ceremonial occasions. In some areas they are the elected leader

What does the council do?

Objective

Understand which services are provided by local government and how the money is raised to provide them.

Getting you thinking

1 Are these services provided where you live?

2 Why do you think local councils provide these services? What would happen if it did not provide them?

Spurley Swimming Pool

Spurley High Secondary School

Lighting up times

12 March: 18.15 – 06.13
13 March: 18.19 – 06.09
14 March: 18.23 – 06.04
15 March: 18.27 – 05.57

24 Starter Homes Due 2004

Pearman's Housing Association with Spurley Council

What does the council do?

Your local council is responsible for a range of services for your community, including education, social services, leisure, planning and transport, housing, fire and the police.

The amount of spending will depend on many different things. Here are some examples:

● If the population of the area is very young, they will need lots of schools.

● If there are many old people, they may need help from social services.

● If there are lots of people, there will be lots of refuse to collect.

A brand new sports centre, for example, is a very expensive item and has to be paid for. The council will work out how much it needs to spend in the coming year and then calculate how much money it must raise.

The council funds schools, which are free. It runs sports centres which are usually cheaper than private clubs. The council provides these services because many people would not be able to afford to pay for them.

Sometimes councils work together with private businesses to run their services. Council houses can be sold to private housing associations, and councils can use the money to repair remaining council property or to build new council housing.

The council has to work out its priorities. It never has the money to provide everything it would like to. Central government does not give the local council a free hand because it sets a limit on how much money can be spent.

When you vote in local elections, you are helping to decide what happens where you live.

Check your understanding

1 What sorts of services do local councils provide?

2 Where do local councils get their money from?

3 Why does central government give more money to some councils than others?

4 Why is it important to vote in local elections?

Find out

1 How does your local council raise and spend its money? You can find out from the town hall, council offices or the library. The council might also have a website with the information.

2 Investigate the work of one of the council's departments.

A local council's income and expenditure

Education £62.3

Social services £37.4

Housing £4.5

Planning and transport £12.8

Fire and police £8.6

Other £6.7

Leisure £8.8

Expenditure

Income

Business rates £45.3 million

Council tax £68

General government grant £26.1

Tax surplus from last year £1.8

? Make a list of services provided by this council. Put them in order according to how much they cost.

? Why does the council spend money on these services?

? If the council decided to spend more on leisure, where might the money come from?

Where does the money come from?

In order to pay for these services, the local council raises money from residents and businesses in the area.

- **Council tax** is paid by all the residents of the area. The amount that each person pays will depend on the value of the house they live in. People who live in big houses will pay more than those who live in small houses.

- **Business rates** are paid by all the local businesses. The amount that is paid depends on the rent that could be charged for the office, shop or factory that the business uses.

Money also comes from central government. The amount depends on the needs of the area and how much can be raised locally. Poorer areas tend to receive more than richer parts of the country.

Central government helps poorer areas more because it is harder for them to raise money locally. If many people are unemployed, houses will tend to have a lower value so the council tax will only bring in a relatively small amount of money. Spending in these areas often needs to be greater as people often need a lot of help from social services.

Key terms

business rates: a form of tax paid by all the businesses in an area. The amount a business pays depends on the rent that could be charged for their premises

council tax: a tax paid by everyone who lives in an area. It is based on the value of their house

Talking to the council

Objective

Understand how people can raise issues with the local council.

Getting you thinking

1 Why do you think Suffolk County Council has put the Graffiti Wall on its website?

2 What advantages are there for the public in communicating with the council in this way?

3 Who do you think the Graffiti Wall might appeal to?

4 Why do you think the council wants to talk to this group of people?

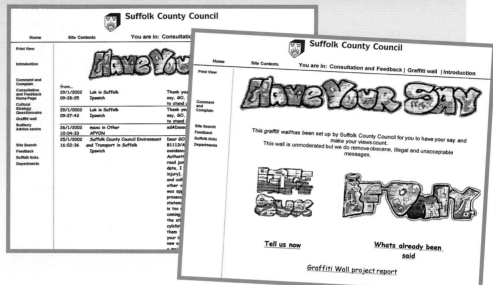

Communicating with the council

Everyone's first line of communication with the local council is at the election. Almost all the population, aged 18 or over, has a vote. The actions of the council between elections will affect people's decisions when it comes to voting.

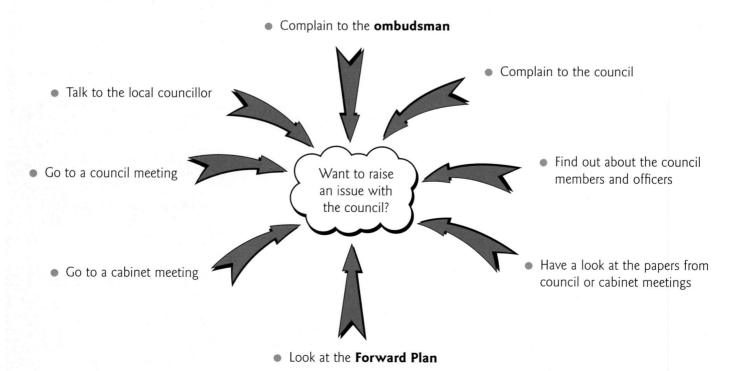

- Complain to the **ombudsman**
- Complain to the council
- Talk to the local councillor
- Find out about the council members and officers
- Go to a council meeting

Want to raise an issue with the council?

- Go to a cabinet meeting
- Have a look at the papers from council or cabinet meetings
- Look at the **Forward Plan**

The way you go about talking to the council will depend on the issue.

- If you want to influence a decision, you need to get to the decision-making process at an early stage. Talking to your councillor is a good start as you can ask advice on how to put across your point of view.

- If you want to find out what is going to happen in the future, ask to look at the Forward Plan as this will set out the general aim of the council's plans.

- If you want to find out about a decision that has been made, have a look at the **minutes** of the cabinet meeting.

A local councillor at his surgery

- If something has gone wrong, you will want to complain. You will probably need to talk to the people employed by the council, but your local councillor will be able to help. If all your complaints fail and you really think the council is in the wrong, you may have to turn to the ombudsman. This is the last resort and you need to have done all you can to get the council to sort out the problem.

More effective?

A lone voice can sometimes seem too quiet to be heard. A group of people who all have the same views can be more effective than one campaigning alone. The campaign might be about aircraft noise, wanting a by-pass, not wanting a by-pass, a new supermarket opening, the lack of facilities for young people or many, many more issues.

Your views count

In Hertfordshire, the county council takes young people's views seriously. A whole section of its website is aimed at communicating with young people.

Not only does it provide lots of information about what's going on, it also has help and advice for young people in the area. And, most important of all, its asks them what they think.

Hertfordshire also has **youth councils** which meet frequently and feed their points of view into the main council, and there are many such groups across the county. A young people's web conference has also been used to hear what young people think.

Check your understanding

1 How often are council elections held?

2 In which ways could you contact the local council in the following situations?
- You notice that the paving stones in your street are becoming cracked and uneven.
- You disagree about plans to build a new supermarket.
- You want to know how much money is going to be spent on education.
- You've heard that a youth centre is going to close down.

Find out

Look at your local council's website. What does it tell you about getting in touch with people at the council? Does it have a young people's section? If not, why not ask them why?

Putting on the pressure

Objective

Find out how pressure groups influence the actions of the council.

Getting you thinking

Give way to oncoming vehicles

I will never forget day when Jay, a boy from the village, was killed. He wasn't the first person to be hit by a car speeding through the village. The council seemed to think that 40mph was quite slow enough – but cars always thought they could get away with more. What we really needed was a 30mph-limit and some rumble strips so everyone noticed.

It was time to act. I started a petition. There were copies in all the local shops, the pub, and with all the local organizations. Soon we had over 5000 signatures and we were ready to make our mark.

I took the advice of our local councillor who suggested that I should go to the council meeting to make my point. I sent a letter and the petition in advance so they would be prepared. At the meeting I stood up and explained what we were asking for. The council members listened carefully.

The council members understood what we wanted and why we wanted it. Within a few months, we, like other villages, had the 30mph-limits that would make our lives safer.

1 Why was it a good idea to:
- organize a petition
- talk to the local councillor
- send a letter and the petition before the meeting
- go to the meeting in person?

Pressure groups

People who have a message that they want to get across often form a **pressure group**. A group of people can often have more effect than a single person if they want something to change. Pressure groups want to influence people in government – local, national and even international.

Pressure groups come in all shapes and sizes, but they are usually concerned with one issue or area of policy. For example, the petition for right of access was started by one person, then other people got involved in order to put pressure

on the local council. They formed a small pressure group, which had one objective. Once the work was done and the group had succeeded in winning the right of access, the group disbanded.

Many pressure groups work on a much larger scale. Famous groups like Greenpeace and Shelter have objectives that might lead them to put pressure on national government and big businesses, as well as activities at a local level.

Getting your voice heard

The key to getting your voice heard is to put together a campaign that reaches as many people as possible.

> **Is there a group of people who care about the issue?**
> *Organize the group and give people responsibilities.*

> **Is the message clear?**
> *Make sure that everyone understands what you are trying to achieve.*

> **Who do you need to talk to?**
> *Find out who is responsible for the things you want to change.*

> **Have you got good evidence?**
> *Do you need a petition to show that lots of people care about the issue? Have you got the facts and figures right?*

> **Is there a local radio station or newspaper?**
> *Local radio stations and papers are always looking for news. How do you get in touch with them?*

> **Can you make your argument more persuasive?**
> *Look at all the material you have. Test it out on people. Make sure that the key points are very clear. Are there any key issues which will make people take notice? Use them!*

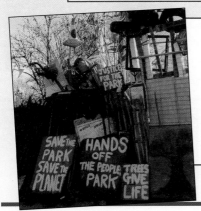

Getting the message across. Different people will need the message in different ways. You might give out leaflets in the high street or put out a press release so the local media know what is happening, prepare a presentation for the council. You will need to fit the method to the audience that you are trying to impress.

Check your understanding

1 Why is a pressure group usually more effective than a single person in getting things changed?

2 What is the aim of pressure groups?

3 Why might a pressure group only exist for a short length of time?

Find out

Is there a local issue that you really care about? Work out what you would do in order to change things.

Discuss

1 Why do you think people get involved in local issues?

2 Why do you think some people don't get involved?

Getting elected

Getting you thinking

"I first got interested in politics when I was at school. A little later I started to think – instead of sitting at home complaining about things like crime, or poverty, or the damage to our environment, why not actually try to do something? So I stood for Parliament, got elected, and now I am working with other MPs on these problems. Politics isn't boring. It's about the stuff of life. It's about who we are as a society, how we govern ourselves and how we treat others on our planet. In our democracy you don't have to be an MP to have your say on these things, you just have to be interested in the world around you."

George Osborne, Conservative MP for Tatton

"I first got involved in politics because I believed that my local area could be better. I wanted to be able to express my views and not rely on others to make the choices. If you don't have your say, others will. That can lead to decisions being taken for the majority of people by a small minority. That's bad for democracy. We should all want to take part in creating the best town, country or world to live in. The very minimum we should do is vote for people who we believe will make those changes.

"Politics may seem boring but it's very important because the decisions that are taken affect every aspect of our lives – what age we can drive, whether we get a good education, what our healthcare system is like, and many more."

Claire Ward, Labour MP for Watford

1 What made George and Claire decide to become MPs?

2 Why do they think people should have their say?

3 What issues do politicians deal with?

4 What could happen if you don't bother to vote?

Becoming a Member of Parliament

There are 659 **Members of Parliament** – or MPs. They have all been elected to represent a part of the country known as a **constituency**. Most MPs were chosen by one of the political parties to be its candidate at an election. If they win the election, they become the MP who represents everyone in the area.

A few people stand as independents and therefore do not go through the party system. A doctor, who was furious that the local hospital was to be closed, stood as an independent and won the seat.

Fighting an election

You have all seen posters everywhere at election time. The campaign starts the minute a **general election** is declared, if not before. The current government tries to choose the best moment to 'go to the country', which is another way of saying 'calling an election'.

To attract voters the political parties and candidates will:

- send out leaflets telling people what they have done in the past and plan to do in future
- go **canvassing**
- attract press coverage
- hold public meetings.

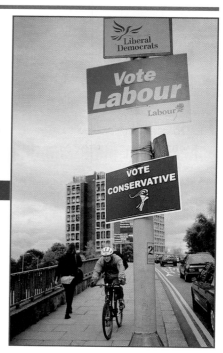

Who shall I vote for?

Voters choose their party for all sorts of reasons.

The media

Newspapers and TV let people know what's going on but they can also affect how people think. Some newspapers always reflect the ideas of one of the political parties while others take a wider view.

Who you know

People's decisions on who to vote for are often affected by their friends and family.

Your religion

Religious belief can persuade people to vote for the party that holds views in line with their own.

Where you live

Political parties often have strongholds in certain areas. For instance, in the south, people have traditionally voted Conservative.

Your age, gender or ethnicity

More young people and ethnic minorities vote Labour. More women used to vote Conservative but the balance has shifted.

Social class

Upper and middle class people have tended to vote Conservative and working class people to vote Labour. This divide has become less rigid as the parties' policies have become more alike and society less class-based.

Party policy and image

People tend to vote for the party rather than their local candidate. The image of the party and the leader has become increasingly important as the role of the media has increased.

When people have taken all these things into account, they will decide who to vote for. Whoever is elected MP is then responsible for representing all people in their constituency in parliament, whichever party they belong to.

A local candidate out canvassing

Check your understanding

1 Do candidates have to represent one of the main political parties? Give reasons.

2 How do candidates try to attract voters?

Find out

1 Who is your local MP? Which political party do they belong to?

2 How many candidates were there at the last election in your constituency? Which parties did they represent? How many votes did they each win?

3 Speak to family members and find out what influences them at election time.

Key terms

canvassing: party members going to try to persuade people to vote for their party in an election

constituency: the area represented by an MP

general election: an election for a new government. In the UK, these take place at least every five years

Member of Parliament: a person who has been elected to represent a constituency in parliament

Part of the system

Getting you thinking

Imagine you are a new MP.

1 What might you think on entering the House of Commons for the first time?

2 Do you think your constituents understand the processes of Parliament?

3 How do you think it might be made easier to follow?

4 Is there anything that you would like to change about the country while you are an MP?

Into power

When a political party wins a general election, it forms a government. The leader usually becomes the **Prime Minister**. His first task is to choose the members of the **Cabinet**. This is the inner circle of people who run the government departments. These include:

- the Treasury, which runs the finances
- the Home Office, which is responsible for law and order
- the Foreign Office, which is responsible for the UK's interests abroad.

The other departments cover:

- health
- education
- trade and industry
- culture, the media and sport
- transport
- environment and food
- defence
- international development.

Wales, Scotland and Northern Ireland also have their own departments.

The people who lead these departments are known as **Secretaries of State**. They have assistants who are called **Ministers of State**. There are also a range of other jobs for non-cabinet MPs in the departments. After the election, MPs wait for a call from the Prime Minister's office, in the hope of getting a job in the government. The first job in a government department is a step to becoming a Minister.

Taking your seat

For a new MP, taking your seat in the **House of Commons** is an exciting event. After what might be years of wanting and waiting to be elected, joining the body that runs the country is a big moment. Here is what they find:

MPs debate new laws and policies in the **House of Commons**. Sometimes debates become furious and the Speaker has to act very firmly to keep things in order. On occasion, an MP can be thrown out of the House of Commons if things get out of hand.

The speaker, who organizes business and keeps order.

Backbenchers who don't have jobs in the Government or Opposition sit on benches at the back.

MPs who don't belong to the main party or largest Opposition party also sit on the Opposition bench.

The government benches: the Prime Minister sits at the front surrounded by the Cabinet.

The opposition benches: the Leader of the Opposition sits at the front surrounded by the **Shadow Cabinet**.

Starting work

MPs have a range of responsibilities.

- The first responsibility is to the people who elected them. There is often a lot of mail from the constituency, which must be dealt with. An MP will hold a frequent 'surgery' in the constituency to listen to people's ideas and worries.

- They take part in debates in the House of Commons and will usually vote with their political party.

- If they have a post in a government department, they will be busy working on government policy and working out new laws.

- They might sit on a committee which keeps a check on the activities of the government departments.

Check your understanding

1 What does a Secretary of State do?

2 What is the responsibility of every MP?

Find out

Does your MP have any responsibilities in government or opposition? If so, what do they do?

Key terms

Cabinet: a group of MPs who head major government departments. It meets weekly to make decisions about how government policy will be carried out

House of Commons: the more powerful of the two parts of the British Parliament. Its members are elected by the public

Minister of State: an assistant to the Secretary of State

Opposition: political parties who are not in power

Prime Minister: the leader of the majority party in the House of Commons and the leader of the government

Secretary of State: an MP who is in charge of a government department such as health or defence

Shadow Cabinet: this consists of the leaders of the main opposition party

What does the government do?

Getting you thinking

Ban hunting!

Raise taxes

Ban hand guns!

Curfew for teenagers!

CUT BENEFITS

Change the licensing laws!

A parliament for Scotland

1 Why do you think a government might want to make laws like these?

2 What do you think would happen if the government passed laws that the population did not like?

3 Why do people, in general, keep the laws which are passed by parliament?

Power

Parliament passes laws that determine how we live our lives. By electing a government, we give it the power to do this. If people break the laws, they can be punished. The government is given authority because the population accepts that an election is a fair way of deciding who will hold power for a five-year period.

The government is **accountable** because it has to answer to the voters. If voters do not like what is happening, the government will not be re-elected.

How are laws made?

Laws go through several stages before coming into force. The government often puts out a **Green Paper**, which puts forward ideas for future laws. Once the ideas have been made final, a **White Paper** is published. This lays out the government's policy. To turn policy into law, the proposals are introduced to parliament in the form of a **bill**. To change the school leaving age, for example, the government would have to introduce an Education Bill. Having gone through the process shown in the diagram on page 73, the bill becomes an Act of Parliament and, therefore, part of the law of the country. The government is accountable to the population so it needs to be sure that everyone has had an opportunity to comment.

It is important that laws are carefully put together, or drafted, because there are always some people who want to find a way of avoiding them. If a law can be interpreted in a different way, it will be very hard to enforce.

Passing through parliament

First reading

The bill is introduced formally in the House of Commons. Before it reaches this stage, it has been worked on by a Drafting Committee to make sure that it is correctly put together. A bill can be many pages long. At this stage there is no debate.

Second reading

A few weeks after the first reading stage, the bill is debated fully in the House of Commons. A vote is taken and if the majority of MPs approve of the bill, it is passed.

Standing committee

A group of 16 to 20 MPs look at the bill carefully and make any alterations that came up at the Second Reading, or which they now think are appropriate.

Report stage

The committee sends a report to the House of Commons with all its amendments. These amendments are either approved or changed. Changes are made when there is a lot of opposition to the bill or if there is strong public pressure to do so.

House of Lords

The bill goes through the same process as in the Commons. If the Lords want to change anything, the bill is returned to the Commons.

Third reading

The amended bill is presented to the House of Commons. A debate is held and a vote is taken on whether to approve it.

Royal assent

Once the bill has passed all its stages in the Commons and the Lords, it is sent to the Queen for her signature. This is really a formality as the Queen would never refuse to sign a bill that had been through the democratic process. The bill then becomes an **Act** of Parliament and part of the law of the country.

Find out

Look at the newspapers or Parliament's website at **www.parliament.uk** to find out what bills are going through at the moment. Choose one of them and debate the issue in class.

Discuss

Choose a new law that you would like to see passed. Put your proposals into a 'bill'. Work out what the opposition is likely to say and prepare your arguments.

Check your understanding

1 What is the difference between a bill and an Act?

2 What sort of things do committees have to pay attention to when making amendments to bills?

3 Why do you think there are so many stages before a law is made?

Key terms

accountable: if you are accountable for something, you are responsible for it and have to explain your actions

Act: a law passed by government

bill: a proposal to change something in law

Green Paper: this puts forward ideas that the government wants discussed before it starts to develop a policy

White Paper: this puts government policy up for discussion before it becomes law

Making a choice

Objective

Understand how the government raises finances and what it spends the money on.

Getting you thinking

"Why are people waiting on trolleys at the hospital?"

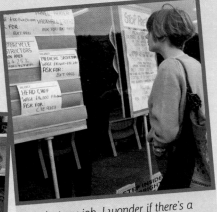

"I've lost my job. I wonder if there's a training course that will help me to get another one?"

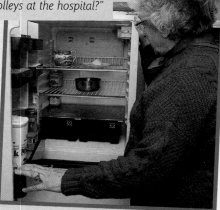

"Is Gran's pension enough to live on?"

"What will it cost to go to university?"

1 What are these people worried about?

2 Make a list of the areas of spending that the questions refer to.

3 Where do you think the money comes from to pay for all these services?

4 Do you think there is a limit to the amount that the government can spend? Why?

5 How should the government decide how to spend its money?

What does the government spend?

The government spends its money on a wide range of services. The pie chart shows the main areas of spending and the proportion spent on each area. The way it is divided up varies a little from year to year but the overall picture stays much the same.

People usually vote for political parties which spend money in ways they like.

How does the government spend its money?

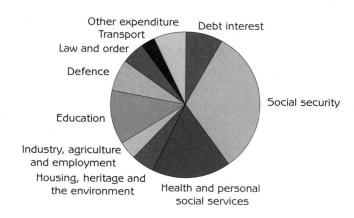

Other expenditure
Transport
Law and order
Defence
Education
Industry, agriculture and employment
Housing, heritage and the environment
Health and personal social services
Debt interest
Social security

Where does the money come from?

If the government is to provide these services, it needs to raise money to pay for them. The money, or **revenue**, comes from taxation or borrowing.

Income tax is not paid by people who earn very little, but as your income rises you pay more tax. It is worked out as a percentage of your earnings. People on higher earnings start to pay a higher percentage of their earnings.

Corporation tax is paid on the profit made by all businesses.

Value added tax is paid on almost everything we buy apart from food, children's clothes, books and newspapers. The amount paid is a percentage (17.5%) of the total value of the goods or services.

Excise duty is charged on a special range of items, many of which are not very good for us if we have too much of them. These include alcohol and cigarettes.

Other taxes include those on cars and petrol. These allow the government to tax particular items to raise money or to try to reduce the amount we buy. Some taxes are raised in the local area. These include council tax and business rates.

Making ends meet

The decisions on taxes and spending happen each year in the **Budget**. The **Chancellor of the Exchequer** is responsible for deciding where the money comes from and how it is spent. The Chancellor works with government departments to decide what is needed and what must come first. It can be difficult to get the right balance because often every department will want to spend more.

Just like everyone else, if the government wants to spend more than its income, it has to borrow. When it borrows, it has to pay interest to the people who lend it money.

Over the years, there has been a steady increase in the amount that governments spend. At the moment, it amounts to about £6000 for each person, each year. People's voting decisions often depend on what the political parties say they will do about taxes and spending if they win the election.

Where does the money come from?

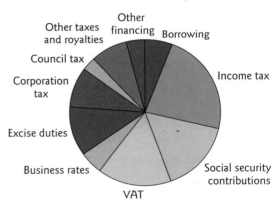

Check your understanding

1 What does the Chancellor of the Exchequer do? Why can this work be difficult?

2 What has been happening to the amount of government spending over the years?

3 Why might government spending influence the way people vote?

Find out

The Treasury is the government department which is responsible for the Budget. Look at its web site at **www.treasury.gov.uk** to find out how the government raises and spends its money. Click on the 'Budget' heading on the site. You will find a summary document which explains the government's spending decisions.

Key terms

budget: this happens every year. The Chancellor of the Exchequer explains how the government will raise and spend its money

Chancellor of the Exchequer: the member of the government who is responsible for the country's finances

government revenue: the money raised by the government

Joining in

Objective

Understand how and why people participate in political parties and pressure groups.

Getting you thinking

Lucy says ...

I joined the Liberal Democrats because I want to make the country I live in a more tolerant place. The Liberal Democrats aim to encourage everybody to make the most of their opportunities and give us the freedom to live our lives the way we wish. The most important issues for me are equality and fairness for all.

Since I have been a member of the Liberal Democrats I have helped in a general election and met lots of other young people with the same interests. Soon I'm off to a weekend organized by Liberal Democrat Youth and Students, which will give me a chance to learn more about the Party and its campaigns.

Lee says ...

Not having a cinema was a big blow for Newbury and it hit young people very hard, as there wasn't much to do. If the cinema was to reopen, action was needed. Working with local councillors and the MP, we launched a petition to show how much the town needed a cinema. We got the local press to cover the launch and it was a great success.

Organizing a campaign with good media coverage taught me how to deal with situations like interviews. It shows prospective employers that I am capable of organizing and carrying out a project. I also felt that I had helped the people of Newbury.

1 How did Lucy and Lee join in? **2** Why did they join in? **3** Do you 'join in'? If so, what do you do and why?

Why join in?

Lucy and Lee joined in because they felt that they could have an effect and help to get things done. People often say 'they' when referring to government, big business and other organizations which they don't think they can affect – "They must do something about". Lucy and Lee decided that they *could* make a difference. They both felt that they got something out of it as well.

What to join?

- **Political parties**
  The major political parties all have youth sections. Organizations encourage young people to take part because they want people to stay committed later on.

- **Pressure groups**
  Pressure groups often work to promote a cause such as looking after the environment, like the World Wide Fund for Nature and Friends of the Earth, or by helping relieve housing problems, like Shelter. Trade union organizations like the Confederation of British Industry are pressure groups which work to protect the interest of their members.

How do pressure groups work?

Pressure groups look for the best ways to get their message across and find support. They might:

- use adverts, press releases, special days or media stunts to put an issue in the public eye
- **lobby** MPs by writing to them, meeting them, organizing petitions and trying to involve them in the work of the organization
- try to influence changes in the law
- sponsor MPs and finance political parties.

The pros and cons of pressure groups

Pro
Pressure groups ...

Provide information for the public

Let governments know what people think

Give a voice to a wide range of views

Represent issues which cross party lines, like capital punishment and abortion

Help people to persuade governments

Represent people without a voice, like the old or the homeless

Keep a check on government, especially when the opposition is weak

Provide public services like legal aid or housing

Con
Pressure groups might ...

Influence governments at the expense of the majority interest

Break the law through their campaigns

Bribe or corrupt MPs to get their way

Influence government leaders and therefore reduce the influence of backbench MPs

Be undemocratic, so a small group of people can decide what is to be done

Have more power than individual voters

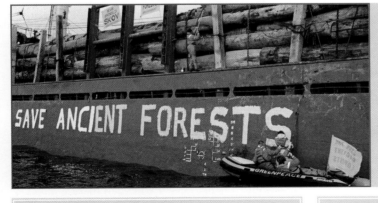

Greenpeace activists painting the ship 'Agia Irene' which was carrying hundreds of African logs from the last surviving tropical ancient forests

Check your understanding

1 What can individuals do if they want to help shape the way things are done?

2 Why could it be argued that pressure groups help democracy? Why could it be said that they harm democracy?

Find out

1 Find out about political youth sections from political party websites.

2 Find out about the work of a national or international pressure group. What are their current campaigns? What successes have they had in the past? How do they encourage individuals to join in with their work?

Discuss

Membership for pressure groups like Greenpeace and Amnesty International is growing, while interest in political parties is declining. Why do you think this is? What could be the negative and positive aspects of this trend?

Key terms

lobby: to try to persuade MPs to support a particular point of view. This used to happen in the 'lobby', or hallway, on the way into Parliament

More democratic?

Objective

Understand that there are changes taking place in the way democracy works.

Getting you thinking

"I voted for my MP but I wouldn't have voted for that new law that's just been passed!"

"But why doesn't Cornwall have a parliament? It's just as different from London as Wales and Scotland."

"Why should people sit in the House of Lords and make decisions about our future, when they haven't been elected?"

1 Why do we vote for MPs rather than everyone voting for every law that is passed?

2 Do you think that other regions of the country should have parliaments? Explain your views.

3 Do you think that the people in the House of Lords should be elected? Explain your views.

How democratic?

Democracy originated in ancient Athens, Greece, where all citizens voted on every issue. This was less democratic than it sounds because only a small proportion of the population were classed as 'citizens'. Women and slaves, for example, were excluded.

In the UK, we elect MPs to represent us. The country is too large for everyone to have their say on all occasions. MPs vote, in general, according to the policy of their political party. MPs can't vote in a way that suits all their constituents because some voted for another political party and hold different views.

When a **referendum** is held every voter can make a direct contribution to a decision. In the UK they are held on topics that have great long-term implications for the country, like joining the Euro. The outcome may be binding or just used to advise the government.

Sometimes MPs are given a 'free vote', which means they don't have to vote with their party. Free votes are usually taken on matters of conscience, such as abortion. MPs will often be lobbied hard by pressure groups that want their support. Constituents may also want their MP to vote in a particular way.

Real democracy?

The House of Lords has always had the role of checking and challenging bills as they pass through the system to become law. It has always included **hereditary peers**, who were only there because they had inherited the role. This was not really a good reason for being involved in ruling the country. There has been pressure to reform the Lords for a long time.

Life peers, who have been appointed by the government or opposition, also sit in the House of Lords. The number of new life peers is controlled by the government. A number of **people's peers** have also been appointed and there are plans for further change but the House of Lords is still not really democratic.

Devolution

The Scottish Parliament and Welsh **Assembly** were both set up following referenda. There had been lengthy campaigns for **devolution** in both countries. People wanted devolution because it shifted some power and authority from London to their own capital cities. Scotland voted strongly for its Parliament, which has the ability to raise taxes and pass laws. The Welsh voted by a narrow margin of 0.6% for their Assembly. It can spend the UK government's allocation of money to Wales, but it cannot set taxes and make laws because it is not a parliament.

Since the formation of Northern Ireland in 1921, there have been many attempts to create some form of government. The current Assembly has powers to control education, health and local government, but the situation is rarely stable.

There are calls for regional assemblies in the rest of the UK. Many people in regions such as Cornwall and the North East feel that their part of the country is distinctive and has different needs from the rest of the UK.

Check your understanding

1 What is the purpose of a referendum? When are they held?

2 What kind of issues are MPs allowed a free vote on? Why?

3 Who can influence MPs when they have a free vote?

4 What's the difference in the amount of power held by the Scottish Parliament and the Welsh Assembly?

5 Why do some people want to have regional governments?

Find out

Are there plans for a regional assembly where you live? If so, what are they?

Discuss

What issues do you think a regional assembly should be responsible for? Are there issues that might be more important in your area than in others?

Key terms

Assembly: a body of people elected to decide on some areas of spending in a region

devolution: the transfer of power from central to regional government

hereditary peers: people who inherited the title 'Lord'

people's peers: people who are selected to sit in the House of Lords

referendum: a vote by the whole electorate on a particular issue

Vote, vote, vote!

Objective

Understand that there are campaigns to encourage people to vote in the UK.

Getting you thinking

1 What's your reaction to this poster? Do you agree that 16-year-olds should be allowed to vote?

2 Think of arguments you would add to the ones in the poster if you were trying to persuade someone that 16-year-olds should be given the vote.

Old enough to pay taxes but not to decide which politicians spend them

Old enough to get married and have kids but not to vote on education policy

Old enough to die for your country but not to elect the people who send you to war

IT'S TIME 16 YEAR OLDS WERE TREATED AS ADULTS Votes@16

Threats to democracy?

In the 2001 General Election, only 60% of the population voted – the lowest number since 1918. Some say that this means the United Kingdom is no longer a very democratic country.

Making your vote count

'First past the post' is the system used for general elections in the UK. People have one vote in one constituency and the candidate with the most votes in each constituency becomes the MP for that area.

If you added all the votes in the country together, sometimes the winning party does not have the most votes. In each constituency, the candidate with the most votes wins, whether the majority is small or large. If the party that wins the most seats has lots of small majorities, the total count may be smaller than the opposition.

When all the constituencies in the country are taken together, the proportion of the votes each party won might not be the same as the proportion of seats each party has in the government. This also makes it hard for small parties to win any seats.

A new system of voting?

Proportional representation, or PR, means that every vote counts. Northern Ireland uses the single transferable vote system (STV) of PR. The constituencies are larger, so each one elects five or six people. Voters put all the candidates in order of preference, putting 1 against their favourite candidate, 2 against their second favourite, and so on. Candidates with the most votes overall win their seats in government.

One issue – one vote

In a referendum you vote on a particular issue so people really feel that they can have an effect. This might encourage more people to vote because they can pick and choose the policies they agree with. It is, however, difficult for a government to plan if referenda are held on every topic.

Persuading people to vote

Party political broadcasts

During the 2001 General Election, about 50% of the population watched party political broadcasts compared with 70% in 1997. In future, it is thought that short American-style election adverts might interest more voters.

The internet

Political parties could use the internet to provide information and organize online surveys of public opinion. People might want to vote if they could join in debates and had easier access to information.

Geri Halliwell appeared in Labour's first election broadcast for the 2001 election. Labour hoped to attract more young voters.

Postal votes
Most people go to a polling station to vote. You can also use a **postal vote** if you register in time.

Online voting
Many people use computers, so it would be quick and easy to use them to vote – whether you were at home or at work.

Making it easier to vote

Convenient location
Most of us go to the supermarket so why not use them as polling stations?

Sunday voting
In many countries elections are held on Sunday. For many people, it is a day off so it would be easier to find the time to vote.

Check your understanding

1 Why might low voter turnout be a bad thing for democracy?

2 What does 'first past the post' mean? How does it affect small parties?

3 Why might proportional representation be a fairer system than 'first past the post'?

4 Comment on the different ways of helping increase participation in elections. Do you think they would be successful? Are there any disadvantages? Give reasons.

Key terms

first past the post: an electoral system where voters have one vote per constituency and the candidate with the most votes wins

postal vote: voters can make their vote by post, rather than by going to a polling station

proportional representation: an electoral system in which the number of seats a party wins is roughly proportional to its national share of the vote

Action

1 How effective do you think campaigns like the one with Geri Halliwell are at attracting young voters?

2 Plan your own campaign to attract young voters and present it to the class.

What is the media?

Getting you thinking

1 Write a sentence for each of these examples of the **media**, explaining how you use them.

2 Put them into groups which show their main use, for example, 'entertainment' and 'information'.

3 Do you believe or trust more of what you learn from one kind of media than from another? Draw up and complete this table with examples of the media.

media	I trust everything	I trust most things	I trust some things	I trust very little
newspapers				
TV				
radio				

4 How do you decide what to trust?

5 What effect does reading, seeing or hearing material that you don't trust have on your views?

Mass media

The media has become a massive industry during the last 50 years. One hundred years ago, newspapers were the only form of information about what was happening in people's locality, the UK and beyond. In days when many people couldn't read, they only knew what people told them.

Today, there is information on every corner in the form of newspapers and magazines. Television is available 24 hours a day. Cable television and the digital revolution have changed things even more. They provide news, entertainment and education, whenever you want it.

Viewers, listeners and readers

Habits change. A hundred years ago, politicians could expect to speak to a packed hall at election time. There was no television so it was the only way people could ever see who they were voting for. Today, the numbers watching party political broadcasts are in decline. Perhaps there is so much exposure that people are no longer curious about who governs them.

As new methods of communication arrive, people move on. When radio was introduced, families would sit around it listening carefully. When television broadcasts

started, radio listening declined. Now we have over 50 television channels so each company has to work extra hard to attract out attention. With more families having the internet at home, television watching may decline. What will come next?

Who does what?

Despite all the changes, people still buy newspapers, books and magazines, listen to the radio and watch television. The choice of media means that we select the ways of finding out information which suit us best. Although the patterns change, most people use most media most of the time. They simply adjust the amount of time they spend on each one.

	1990	1993	1996
Watching TV	99	99	99
Listening to the radio	96	96	96
Reading books	62	65	65

Annual Abstract of Statistics 2001, ONS

Products for people

All forms of media aim to provide what the customer wants. There are television channels that are aimed at young people and others at an older population.

There is also a growing number which are aimed at people with specific interests ranging from music to gardening and cooking to history.

A source of power?

Giving people information can be a source of power. The decision about what to tell and what not to tell means that you can affect the way people think. When people vote in an election, they are making decisions that affect the country for the next five years. How do they make their voting decisions? Very often, they are based on information from the media. The media therefore helps people to make decisions. If it is not accurate, the effect can be very damaging. If the media presents what it wants people to know, rather than the whole truth, it is difficult for people to make informed decisions.

The following pages explore reasons why the media does not always present the whole truth and why the freedom to communicate is important for democracy.

Find out

1 Look at a range of papers from the same day. Do they tell the stories in different ways? How are they different?

2 Watch the news on television on the same day. Does it give the same picture? Do different channels take a different approach?

3 Do you prefer one newspaper's or television channel's way of telling the story? Do you believe one more than the other? Explain why.

Check your understanding

1 What is meant by the media?

2 How has the media changed over the last 100 years?

3 What does the media provide?

4 Why is the media powerful?

Key terms

media: ways of communicating with large numbers of people

Why should the press be free?

Getting you thinking

> **"The worst-ever attack on the liberties of the people."**
>
> *A member of the Zimbabwean parliament*

International journalist arrested

The Independent newspaper's Zimbabwe reporter has been arrested under new laws. His house had been ransacked and he was told that the order for his arrest had come from the highest level in the government.

1 Feb 2002

Zimbabwe – laws passed which:

- only allow foreign journalists into country to cover specific events
- only allow registered journalists to work
- require media organizations to be registered
- stop people criticizing the President
- limit publication of important information
- stop stories that discriminate against a political party
- only allow demonstrations that have government approval.

Zimbabwe was in the run up to an election when these laws were passed.

1 What did these laws prevent?

2 Why do you think the government brought them into force?

3 What effect do you think it had on the results of the election?

4 Explain why the laws were seen as "the worst-ever attack on the liberties of the people".

5 Why is it important for the media to be free to tell stories?

6 Do you think there should be any limit on what the media can say?

What is freedom?

'Everyone has the right to the freedom of opinion and expression; this right includes freedom to hold opinions without interference and to seek, receive and impart information and ideas through any media, regardless of frontiers.'

Universal Declaration of Human Rights

One of every human being's rights is to have their say. If they don't like the government, they should be free to say so. If people think the government should spend more or less on health, education or defence, laws should not prevent them. If people want to know what is going on, they should be free to find out. Information and data should not be kept secret unless there is a good reason. In a democracy, people need to be able to hear others' points of view and know what is going on if they are to use their vote effectively.

Why control the press?

If information is kept from people, they will find it hard to decide whether the government is keeping its promises or breaking the law in order to stay in power. If a government is determined to stay in power, preventing people from knowing the truth can be very effective. **Censorship** means that people will only know what you want them to know.

Press freedom is often the first thing to go when the government of a country wants to prevent democracy working. A country that controls the press cannot really be democratic. There are examples throughout history. In the last century, the Soviet Union controlled all forms of media. Even today, there are no free television channels in Russia, as part of the former Soviet Union is now known. China also has strong controls on what the people are told. There are examples of press control throughout the world.

Is it ever right to control the media?

When the UK was fighting Argentina over the Falkland Islands in 1981, there was a complete news blackout. Every night a government spokesman appeared on the television and gave a report. He read a message in a slow, serious manner, telling us what the government thought we should know.

When people are caught spying, very often much of the information that is provided in court is not published.

These are both examples of occasions when national security is thought more important than press freedom. Sometimes, by telling people everything you may be giving the game away.

There is, however, always a debate about how much information should be given out.

During the Falklands Conflict, John Nott, the government spokesman, gave reports on the war. Should people be told everything that is going on?

Check your understanding

1 What does the Universal Declaration of Human Rights have to say about press freedom?

2 Why might a government that wants to be re-elected decide to control the press?

3 Why can democracy not work effectively if the press is controlled?

4 Are there reasons why press freedom should sometimes be limited? Why?

Discuss

"The press should have its say." Draw up a list of issues that you think the press should be free to discuss and any that you think it should not be allowed to print stories about. Use your list to frame a law on press freedom.

Key terms

censorship: limiting the information given to the general public

press freedom: the ability of the press to give information and express opinions without control

Legal, decent, honest and truthful?

Getting you thinking

1 Identify the different sorts of people in these pictures.

2 What sorts of thing does the press do to give people cause for complaint?

3 Do you think that complaints are always justified?

4 Make a list of things you feel the press should not do.

5 Make suggestions about how to stop the press doing this sort of thing?

What are the rules?

Anyone in the public eye can be pestered by the press. People find themselves being looked at through the long lens of a camera and on the front page the next day. Ordinary people who have had some good luck or experienced misfortune are just as vulnerable as the famous.

The Press Complaints Commission attempts to prevent this invasion of privacy but it is not always successful. It has drawn up the **Press Code** as guidance for **journalists** working in the media. Although it can look at complaints and decide if the code has been broken, it can do little to prevent it happening again.

The Press Code

Newspapers

- must not publish inaccurate, misleading or distorted information or pictures
- must give a right to reply to any inaccurate reporting
- must respect people's private and family life
- must not harass people for information
- must not intrude on grief or shock
- must not intrude on children during their schooling
- must not use hidden bugs to find things out
- must avoid prejudice
- must not make payments to people involved in criminal cases
- must not profit from financial information
- must not identify victims of sexual assault
- must protect confidential sources

Press Complaints Commission

The wrong side of the law?

Sometimes it's a question of invading people's privacy, but on other occasions the media gets its facts wrong. When this happens a paper or television channel can find itself in court facing a **libel** or **slander** case.

Laws prevent anyone from making public statements about people that are not true. Footballers have challenged people who said they fixed a game, politicians have challenged newspapers which said they received money for asking particular questions in parliament. *Private Eye*, the magazine that takes a satirical look at the world, often finds itself in court because it has pushed the limits too far.

Tabloid or broadsheet?

People buy four times as many tabloid papers as broadsheets. Their size is not the only difference between them. The broadsheets tend to take a more serious view of the world and their headlines reflect this. In contrast, on days when dramatic world events are taking place, tabloid papers have been famous for headlining footballers, sex and money.

Average sales of most popular daily newspapers in the UK (August 2001)

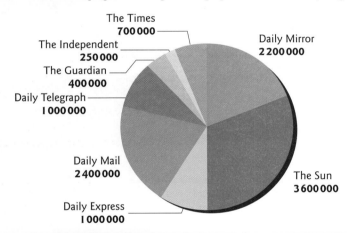

The Times **700 000**
The Independent **250 000**
The Guardian **400 000**
Daily Telegraph **1 000 000**
Daily Mail **2 400 000**
Daily Express **1 000 000**
Daily Mirror **2 200 000**
The Sun **3 600 000**

Legal limits

Just like anyone else, the media has to obey laws about decency. Both discrimination and pornography are against the law and some parts of the media have to be very careful not to overstep the limits.

The tabloids find themselves in front of the Press Complaints Commission or in court more often that the broadsheets. But who is responsible? After all, the more lurid the story, the more we buy.

Find out

1 What decisions has the Press Complaints Commission made recently? Do you agree with their findings? Why?

2 Look at the headlines on a range of newspapers on the same day. How do the broadsheets and tabloids compare? You will find newspapers on the internet as well as in newsagents.

Check your understanding

1 How should people's privacy be protected?

2 How effective do you think the Press Complaints Commission is? Can you think of any examples when their rules have been broken?

3 Why is it important for journalists to protect confidential sources of information?

4 How do broadsheet papers differ from the tabloids?

5 How does the law limit what newspapers can print?

Discuss

1 If people always want to be in the public eye, should they complain when the press invades their lives?

2 We buy more papers when they are full of stories about famous people. Should we hold ourselves responsible when the press invades people's privacy?

Key terms

journalist: a person who gathers news and produces reports for the media

libel: writing incorrect things about people

Press Code: guidelines for the media and journalists about the information they gather and how they gather it

slander: saying incorrect things about people

What news?

Getting you thinking

1 Which media company owns the most papers?

2 Which companies also have a share in television companies?

3 If the people who run the companies have strong views, what effect might this have on the news in the papers and on television?

4 Why do you think the government limits the number of papers and television stations that can be owned by one company?

Who owns the papers?

News Corp.
The Times   Sunday Times   The Sun
News of the World   A large part of BskyB

Trinity Mirror
The Mirror   Sunday Mirror   Sunday People

Daily Mail and General Trust
The Daily Mail   Mail on Sunday
London Evening Standard
20% share of Independent Television News

Guardian Media Group
The Guardian   The Observer

Independent News and Media
The Independent
The Independent on Sunday

Hollinger New Telegraph New Media
The Daily Telegraph

Where does the power lie?

A newspaper or television news programme can choose the stories it wants to tell. It can also decide how to tell the story. The owners of a paper appoint an **editor** to run it for them. The editor has the power to make these decisions. Often, an editor is chosen because they have the same points of view as the owners – so the way the news is presented reflects the owner's point of view. Television news has editors too. They put the programme together in just the same way.

Most newspapers are in the hands of companies which are owned by shareholders. The objective is to make a profit so sales are a top priority and lots of sales means lots of advertising. Businesses that want to sell their products will buy space in papers with many readers. A large proportion of the costs of running a paper come from selling space for advertising. Commercial television is just the same.

All these factors combine to make newspapers and television very powerful.

Who buys what?

Most people read a paper which agrees with their own views. Conservative voters often buy *The Telegraph* or *The Express*, while Labour voters might buy *The Guardian* or *The Mirror*. The way the news is presented depends on the views of the papers. The cartoons are often the give-away. They are always ruder about the party they don't support!

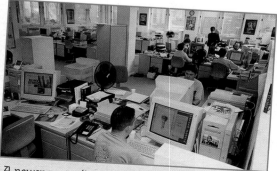

A newspaper editorial office

The influence of advertising

Advertising pays for commercial television and the papers. What would you do if, as editor, you were faced with a story which showed one of your main advertisers in a bad light?

Would you:

- run it?
- hold it over for a day when there were no adverts from that business?
- rewrite the story so it was less critical?
- just ignore it?

It's a tough decision to make.

In a spin?

Politicians often want to be at the top of the news and shown in a good light. Political parties employ **spin doctors** who write the stories and work hard to get them in the news. A common story is about new government spending on health, education or other areas which people care about. When journalists look carefully, however, they often find that the spending has been announced several times before! This is often the work of spin doctors.

Whose views?

Everyone has a point of view which is often hard to hide. If, as a reader or viewer, you are aware of the **bias** of a television programme or newspaper, you can take it into account. If not, you may just believe it all. In a country where only one point of view is permitted, people are unlikely to know what is really going on.

Under control

Every time one media company wants to take over another, the plans are reviewed. If the takeover puts too much power in too few hands, it won't be allowed to go ahead. When Granada bought United's television stations, it was told that HTV would have to be sold, otherwise Granada would have had too much power.

London Weekend
Yorkshire
Meridian
Tyne Tees
Border
Anglia
Granada TV

Who does Granada own?

Check your understanding

1 What does an editor do?

2 Why are media owners powerful?

3 What factors influence the contents of a newspaper?

4 How is media ownership controlled?

Discuss

Do you think democracy is in danger if:

- the media is owned by a small group of people?
- the media can be influenced by business and politicians?

Give reasons.

Find out

Compare stories in two newspapers. Is there a difference in the way the stories are told?

Key terms

bias: to favour one thing over another unfairly

editor: the person who is responsible for the content of a newspaper or television or radio programme

spin doctor: someone who tries to make bad news sound better

TV: information or entertainment?

Getting you thinking

1 Which channels do you think the man is most likely to be looking for? Why?

2 Draw up a pie chart showing the different sorts of television you watch. Explain your choices.

3 What would persuade you to change your viewing habits?

What's on the telly?

Most people have four or five television channels to watch. An increasing number have 100. The introduction of satellite and cable television has shifted people's viewing patterns considerably. If you want to watch sport or cartoons all day, you can! Equally, if you want to watch what's going on in parliament all day, you can do that too.

All the television channels are in competition with each other. Ones with advertising have to show they have lots of viewers if they are to sell advertising time. The BBC is funded by the license fee. We pay to watch it, but questions are asked if viewing figures fall. As viewing numbers are so important, television companies will put out the programmes that they think lots of people want to see.

More channels mean more opportunities for specialist interests because production costs are falling. Nickleodeon, for example, comes from an office in a side street in London. All it needs is a small studio and the ability to run recorded programmes.

All this airtime can have several effects:

- minority interests can be catered for
- information can be provided in different ways for different people
- quality falls because channels have to fill the time.

Which one will you watch? Why?

What goes on in parliament?

Television cameras have only recently been allowed in the Houses of Parliament. Rules were set up about where the cameras were put, who could be filmed and what was to be avoided. For instance, they are not allowed to film an MP who has fallen asleep during a long debate! Output is carefully monitored to give 'a balanced, fair and accurate' picture of the views of all political parties.

When broadcasting began, there was lengthy coverage and few people watched. There are still daily, live programmes but it is now used mainly for news highlights and special events.

Two websites, cable and satellite TV have continuous coverage. These are mainly watched at moments when big issues are being debated and by people who have particular interests in the day's events. It gives access to the UK's parliament to people all round the world.

The whole story?

Almost everyone can vote at 18. Which box to tick on a ballot paper is an important decision because your vote will help to determine the party that controls the country for the next five years. How will you decide? What your friends do? What your parents say? Or will you think about it and come to your own decision?

Television and radio can help you to know what's going on so you can make a decision for yourself. Listening to both sides of a discussion will help you to decide. Only 1% of terrestrial television's output is news, politics or about what's happening to the economy – viewing figures among the young are low.

Is it for me?

Age	Percentage of TV watching time spent watching the news
4–15	9
16–24	10
25–34	12
35–44	14
45–54	16
55–64	18
65+	19

Social Trends 2000, ONS

How can young people be persuaded to watch television news?

What's the message?

Many television programmes have information that is useful for Citizenship. For example, there is plenty of material on sustainable development (see page 116). The workings of business and the economy are often part of the story in drama programmes. Even soaps can help you to think about how communities work. They often help you to understand because they show you real situations where people are affected by what's going on.

Check your understanding

1 What are the advantages of having more television channels?

2 How can television and radio help you to decide who to vote for?

3 Why do you think it is important for television coverage of parliament to be 'balanced, fair and accurate'?

Find out

When you are watching television, make a note of all the incidents which refer to issues relating to Citizenship.

Discuss

1 Why do you think there is so little coverage of news and current affairs in the television?

2 If people only watch entertainment programmes, does this affect their ability to make decisions about who to vote for in an election?

Action

Before elections, all the main parties are given air time to put their message over. Many people think this is a good moment to make a cup of tea! Devise a party political broadcast that would keep people watching.

Can you say what you like?

Getting you thinking

1 Why can the ease of access to the internet mean people might be shocked by what they see?

2 Do you think anyone should be able to put anything on the internet? If not, what do you think should be controlled?

3 If material on the internet is controlled, are there situations in which people might not get the information they need to make decisions, for example, during elections?

Find out – about anything?

There is little to prevent anyone putting anything on the web. It is often hard to track just where material comes from. You will be in trouble, however, if you download information that breaks the law of the country where you live. People's use of the internet has been used to prove their guilt in cases from terrorism to paedophilia. Even at work, staff have been sacked for breaking the rules on downloading unacceptable materials and sending the wrong sort of emails.

All laws about what can and can't be published in other media apply to material on the internet, providing the source of information can be tracked.

Free access?

The Freedom of Information Act, which will be in action fully by 2005, allows everyone to see their personal records. It also means that all information held by public bodies will have to be available. There is already a great deal of government information available on the web. Every government department and local authority has its website to inform the population about what is going on. But remember, whatever you see on the web may be there to persuade you rather than just give you information.

Free for all?

Many websites started out by offering free services to their visitors. Once people had grown used to using them, many started to charge for the service. *The Times*, for example, used to allow free access to all past newspapers but now, if you want to download an article, there is a charge. As the web moves on, charging for information that people really want is likely to become more common.

The internet for citizens

Households with internet access

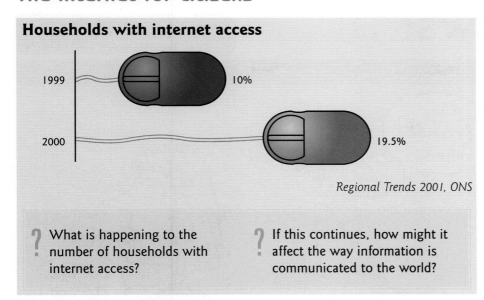

1999 — 10%

2000 — 19.5%

Regional Trends 2001, ONS

? What is happening to the number of households with internet access?

? If this continues, how might it affect the way information is communicated to the world?

People need to be informed if they are to participate. The internet can provide information, ideas, views and opportunities to discuss. All the political parties have their websites, and broadcasters can keep you up to date on what's going on.

In countries where information isn't free, the internet can help people to know what is going on in the rest of the world. In some countries where the government really wants to limit information, they limit internet access.

Key terms

Freedom of Information Act: a law which gives open access to information about individuals, business and government

Find out

Choose a website you would like to know more about and decide how reliable it is. Who wrote it? Is it up-to-date? Is there any bias?

China's solution

In China, the government works hard to control access to the internet. All content providers must register with them and are issued with a license if their material is acceptable. The government controls access to the internet and has strict rules about religious and political information. There are harsh penalties for anyone who breaks the rules.

Know what you're looking at

Not all websites are quite what you think they are. Some people want to influence the views of others by putting convincing-looking information on the web. The motive may be to persuade people to accept or believe in their views. Unless you are careful, you can be taken in.

Check your understanding

1 What are people not allowed to put in print? Look back at previous pages.

2 How can access to the internet be controlled?

3 How is the use of material on the internet controlled?

4 How can a country limit access to the internet?

5 How can the internet help people to be more informed citizens?

Discuss

Should anyone be free to:
● put whatever they want on a website?
● read whatever they want on the internet?

Work out both sides of the argument for each question and come to a conclusion.

Whose views?

Getting you thinking

1 How are all these people making decisions?

2 What problems are there in making decisions in these ways?

3 Do you think there are better ways of making decisions?

4 Draw some bubbles with statements which you think might help them to make more informed decisions.

Subject to persuasion?

We are all subject to persuasion – but we need to look in the right places to be persuaded. People very often read the newspaper that agrees with their views and switch channels on TV when they hear messages that contradict their own ideas. They don't even hear the other side of the story.

There are all sorts of decisions that are made about where you live, your school life or your social life. If the decisions are to be sensible, there are all sorts of points of view that need to be taken into account. Remember Joe, on page 58, who wanted to fight the council when it closed the skate park? The council had listened to the neighbours who complained about the noise and the people who wanted to spend more money on other things, but it hadn't consulted the users of the skate park.

Stories like this are often reported in the local paper. Can you imagine what it would be like if the press could only report the council's point of view and nobody was allowed to challenge it. What effect would this have on people's views?

What information?

More and more information is available to us. The government collects masses of data which are put together by the Office of National Statistics. You'll find lots on its website. The Freedom of Information Act also allows access to a wide range of information about people, businesses and government.

The **Data Protection Act**, however, prevents information that is stored on computers being given out freely. The Human Rights Act may limit information that can be published about people.

There is a balance between helping people to find information and limiting the information that is available.

94

Opinions for the public?

The media is full of **opinion polls**. Questions are asked about all sorts of topics from love to politics. When elections are looming, pollsters are out in force and the results of their surveys are published almost daily. "Are voters changing their minds?" is the first thought of many journalists.

The use of opinion polls has been questioned. If one party, according to the polls, is very popular, its supporters might not vote on election day because they may assume enough people will vote anyway. The party that is behind often fears that more voters will desert the sinking ship. If a poll shows that the parties are very close, it can be misleading because it is hard to get it exactly right.

In some countries, these fears have led to the publication of opinion polls being banned in the last weeks before an election.

Keeping a balance

| schoolchildren | roads/transport system | medical staff | patients | housing | tax payers |

Whenever people have to come to a decision, they need to listen to a variety of points of view. These are often talked of as the views of **stakeholders**, or people who have an interest in the decision. If you ask, "Should the government spend more on health?", you have to think about the patients and medical staff, as well as the people who will receive less funding or the tax payer who will pay more tax. They are all stakeholders. A search through the media often provides the material you need to decide for yourself.

Key terms

Data Protection Act: this Act limits the way that information stored on computers can be used

opinion poll: questioning a sample of the population to build a picture of the views of the public on a particular topic

stakeholders: people who have an interest in a decision that is being made

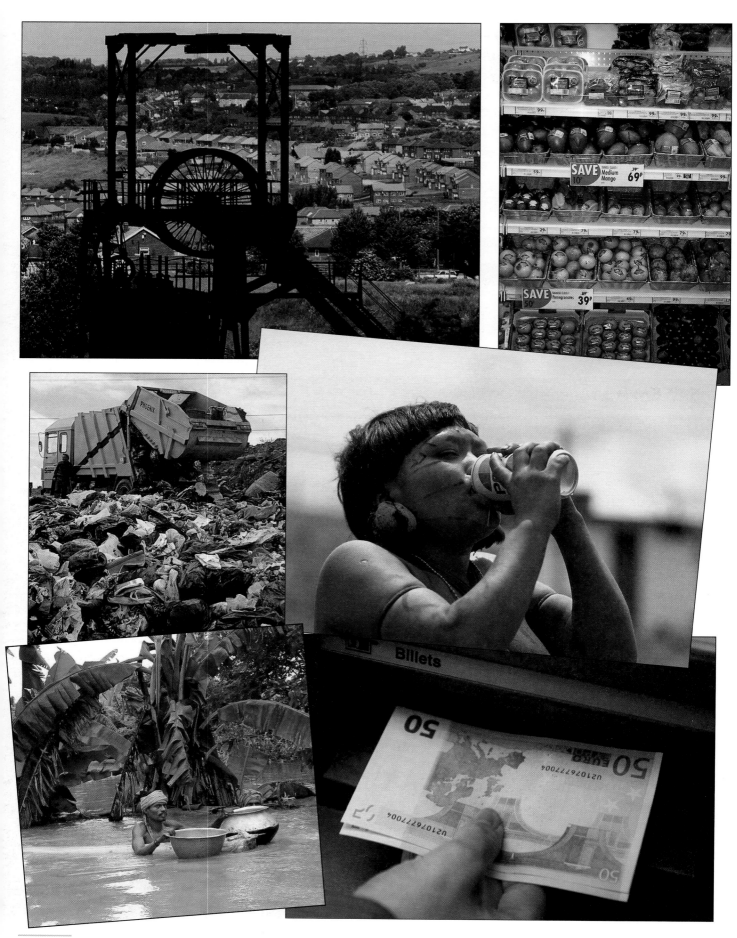

Theme 3 The global village

What is an economy?

Getting you thinking

1 How many of these people provide a product or service that we might buy or use?

2 List those which you think are supplied by the council or government.

3 Do any of the above provide goods or services without getting paid?

4 How many are consumers of goods and services?

5 Which of them do you think currently need more financial support?

I work for Carphone Warehouse selling mobile phones.

I'm a builder. I've just completed laying out the new Blockbuster shop in town. I'm also a local councillor.

In my role as council Environmental Health Officer, I make sure restaurants meet health and safety standards.

I'm on a part-time health and beauty course at college. I also work part-time for McDonald's.

I'm a nurse and I also coach junior rugby for my local amateur club.

I'm on a modern apprenticeship, training to be an electrician. I also help with the Samaritans.

I've just set up my own computer repair business. I hope to recruit extra staff soon.

I'm a secretary working for Oxfam.

I'm a retired teacher, but keep busy as a school governor and local organizer for Greenpeace.

What is an economy?

Everyone in the United Kingdom is part of the economy as a consumer, producer or citizen.

● We are all consumers: whatever our age, we buy the products of business.

● Some of us are producers who help make products or provide services. That includes the part-time employee for McDonald's, as well as the secretary working for Oxfam.

The **economy** is measured by adding up either the value of everything that is produced, or the value of everything consumed, in one year. Both calculations should come to the same amount. For the UK in 2000, this figure reached over £800 billion. This works out at over £13 000 per person and about £40 000 per employee per year.

Private and public sector

Most of the things we buy are made by businesses in the **private sector**. These businesses are run by individuals or shareholders. A shareholder owns part of the company but leaves its organization to its managers. The main objective of businesses in the private sector is to make a **profit** for their owners, but the private sector also includes charities that raise money for good causes.

The rest of the economy is owned or run by the government and local councils. This is called the **public sector**. It includes social services, fire and police, education, defence, law, community and sports centres, housing and transport. A key objective for the public sector is to satisfy local residents. If it fails to do so, the political party that controls the council may not be re-elected at the next election.

What effect does competition have on business?

The power of competition

The economy is fired by people wanting to buy things. Businesses will provide these things if there is a profit to be made. If consumers buy less of a product, less will be produced. The resources that were used to make it may be used by another business for another purpose. Food shops in town centres have closed because people use out-of-town supermarkets. The empty shops – the resources – are now used by other businesses, like mobile phone shops. Businesses want to make a profit and will look for new opportunites.

Is it fair?

People who don't have enough money to pay for things they need and want, won't be able to have them.

If everything is provided by the private sector, many people will suffer. If you can't afford education and are in poor health, it can be difficult to find a job and do the things other people do.

As a result, the government provides these and other social benefits. Some are free for all – others are provided according to need. We pay taxes to cover the costs of these and other services.

What would happen if everyone had to pay for healthcare?

Check your understanding

1. How can you work out what the economy is worth in a year?

2. What makes up the economy?

3. What is the difference between the private sector and the public sector?

4. Why do we need the public sector?

5. Why do the government and local councils collect taxes?

Find out

Do a survey of 10 people you know to find out how they contribute to our economy. You could ask whether they produce goods or services. Do they work in the private or public sector? What have been their major purchases over the past year?

Discuss

Should we pay taxes?

Key terms

economy: this is made up of all the organizations that provide goods and services, and all the individuals and organizations that buy them

private sector: this section of the economy is made up of businesses or organizations that are owned by individuals or by shareholders

profit: the money that you gain when you sell something for more than you paid for it or than it cost to make

public sector: is made up of organizations owned or run by the government and local councils

Who does what?

Objective

Understand how people and resources are organized to produce goods and services, and that businesses are interdependent.

Getting you thinking

1 How many businesses are shown on the map?

2 Which businesses either support or depend on others?

3 Some businesses are similar, which means they are in competition with each other. Which businesses are these?

4 Estimate how many employees you think this shopping centre has.

5 Which parts of the shopping centre might the council be involved in.

Larkhill shopping centre

Small businesses

The Larkhill local shopping centre is full of businesses run by individual people. All sorts of businesses can be sole traders, for example, farms, newsagents, dentists, accountants and printers. They all provide a service or products for which people are prepared to pay.

In order to survive, businesses need to make a profit. This means their income from sales must be more than the money they spend on things such as wages, rent and buying stock. These payments out are called costs. A business makes a loss if more money is spent running it than it receives from its customers. If a business keeps making losses, it will collapse.

These businesses need each other. Jill needs suppliers to provide her shop with stock. If the suppliers fail to deliver the newspapers on time, Jill will not be able to provide what the customers want, and 'Jill's Newsagents' will lose business. Suppliers depend on newsagents because they sell their stock. The two businesses are **interdependent**.

Interdependency

Many businesses are dependent on each other. Here are a few of the links to 'Jill's Newsagents':

- *The bus company allows customers to travel to Larkhill.*

- *Local bank for loans and paying in cash from sales.*

- *Suppliers of local and national newspapers, magazines and confectionery.*

- *Local window cleaner cleans the shop windows every week.*

- *Electricity suppliers.*

Specialization

Journalists, photographers, editors, advertising staff, designers, etc., to lay out newspapers

Printers to produce the newspaper or magazine

Transport to distribute product to newsagents

Newsagents

There are many different jobs involved in making a product. The flow chart shows how a newspaper reaches the customers.

Each stage needs different types of people to do different jobs – the printers know how to print and the designer is an expert in design. The distributors need drivers and the newsagents have close contact with their customers who want to buy the paper. All the people and businesses involved are **specialized** in the type of work they do.

Division of labour

If one person did all the jobs needed to sell newspapers they would have to write the articles, design the pages, print the paper, take it to a shop and sell it. The newspaper would take far too long to produce and it would be of low quality. It's much quicker and more efficient in costs and quality if each stage is carried out by people who are expert in their field. This is known as **division of labour**.

Check your understanding

1 Choose a small business in your local area and list as many of its links as you can.

2 Why do you think you have specialist teachers in your secondary school, but a class teacher in your primary school?

3 What different types of non-teaching jobs are there in your school?

4 Why would your school be less well run if your teachers had to carry out all the tasks currently done by non-teachers?

5 What kinds of division of labour are there in a restaurant?

Find out

1 Choose a small shopping area or small industrial estate near you and make a simple map of the businesses there.

2 Show how one of the businesses uses division of labour and/or specialization to be more efficient.

Key terms

division of labour: where employees concentrate on a particular task or job at which they are expert

interdependent: where businesses need each other to survive

specialized: where employees or businesses concentrate on tasks that they can do well

Sharing success or failure

Objective

Understand the consequences of success and failure of businesses on individuals, communities and beyond.

Getting you thinking

'We pride ourselves in giving our customers simple impartial advice.'

Carphone Warehouse started trading in 1989 and now has over 1050 stores in 15 countries, and employs over 5500 people. Its sales income is over £1.1 billion and grew by nearly 60% in 2000.

"I would have been amazed to be told that, within 15 months of joining the company, I would be managing a superstore" – Julie Checkley, Area Sales Manager

The Carphone Warehouse also actively supports charity work.

1 In what ways can the business claim to be successful?

2 How might Carphone Warehouse be contributing to the economy?

3 What evidence is there to suggest that Carphone Warehouse could be a good employer?

Carphone Warehouse: number 21 in the Sunday Times 'Top UK Companies to Work For in the Year 2000' survey

Going for growth

At Carphone Warehouse, success comes from the growing market for mobile phones and providing good customer service. The mobile phone business is very competitive so Carphone Warehouse has to invest in new buildings and equipment so that they keep ahead of competitors. It also needs to employ, train and motivate the staff.

Supporting individuals

Businesses can support the individuals who work for them. Employees receive incomes and training to develop their skills. Many of these skills are transferable. Individuals will be able to use – or transfer – these skills, such as good customer service, to a new job.

Supporting communities

Employees will help local businesses by spending some of their income in local shops, pubs, cafés and restaurants.

Businesses pay taxes from their profits and people pay taxes from their earnings. They also pay tax when they buy things. These taxes provide the government and local councils with money that can be used to benefit the community.

Supporting the wider community

A growing business helps to create or support jobs in other, interdependent, businesses. These jobs may be in the local community, but others might be further away. A growing business will do things like:

- communicate more
- use more energy and water
- buy extra equipment such as computers
- buy more materials from suppliers
- buy more services from other businesses

All these contributions help the country's economy to grow. Successful businesses often create jobs and pay more taxes so people benefit.

Markets moving on

The market for UK coal moved on – that is to say, it changed. Two reasons for this are:

- Oil and gas are often cheaper and cleaner alternatives
- Coal from other countries is cheaper.

When markets move on, people may lose their jobs. Some of the businesses that supported the declining industry will either close down or look for new markets in an attempt to survive. Local shop traders will lose out because people have less money to spend.

Those employees made **redundant** may have the wrong skills for new types of businesses. New businesses are unlikely to start up in areas where people don't have the skills they need, or where other businesses are failing.

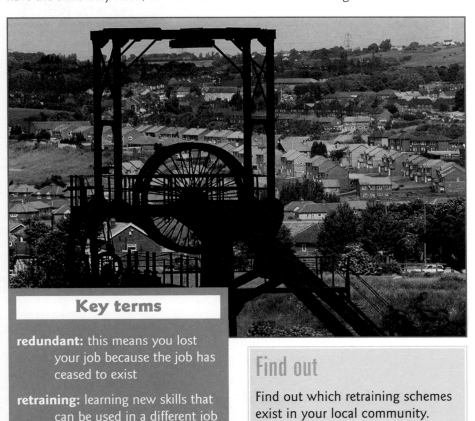

Markets failing communities

The market system is said to have failed a community when unemployment is much higher than in other parts of the country.

Economic decline and growth

It is natural for some businesses to grow and others to decline. The market system brings about a shift of resources towards making things that are most in demand. The economy will grow if the value of the new sales of the expanding businesses is greater than the value lost from declining businesses. If it is the other way round, however, the economy is declining.

Where this happens, the government needs to step in to help. By introducing **retraining** schemes, and investing in roads and other communications, it can make areas where lots of people are unemployed more attractive to new businesses.

Key terms

redundant: this means you lost your job because the job has ceased to exist

retraining: learning new skills that can be used in a different job

Find out

Find out which retraining schemes exist in your local community.

Check your understanding

1 How can an employee benefit from working for a business?

2 How might growing businesses create jobs both in the local community and beyond?

3 How do businesses and their employees provide money for local services?

4 What knock-on effects might there be when a big employer in a local community closes down?

5 How might the government reduce the impact of a big employer closing down?

6 What would happen if more business were closing down than expanding in the country?

When prices rise

Objective

Understand what causes inflation, the problems of inflation and how it might be controlled.

Getting you thinking

The changing value of money

£1000 in 1971 would buy as much as £8609 in 2001

£1000 in 1981 would buy as much as £2335 in 2001

£1000 in 1991 would buy as much as £1308 in 2001

1 What happens to the value of money over time?

2 If a small car cost £1000 in 1971, what might you expect to pay for it today?

3 What do people expect to happen to their pay?

What would this type of car cost today?

How does inflation happen?

Inflation happens when things we buy get more expensive as time passes. It often comes about because people want to spend more. In fact it's one big circle:

Businesses want to provide extra goods and services so they buy new equipment and buildings and recruit more people.

People demand more goods and services.

As businesses continue expanding it becomes more difficult for them to employ new staff, and buy land and materials. All these resources are limited – there is only a certain amount of land, material and employees available.

Businesses must pay higher wages to attract the staff from other businesses. Rents for properties go up because of increased competition for space.

As people have the money to buy more things, they are prepared to pay higher prices so businesses can pass on these higher costs.

Who is affected by rising prices?

People who save will lose out – the value of their savings will not buy so much in the future.

People with incomes that do not grow at the rate of inflation will also lose out. This will include pensions that are not linked to the inflation rate.

Borrowers will gain because the value of their debt will fall.

UK businesses can also lose out if inflation in other countries is at a lower rate. The price rises make our products and services more expensive to buy.

Can it go too far?

If prices rise too far, businesses start losing money because people stop buying their products. To stay in business, companies cut their costs by making people redundant. This may keep the business going, but unemployment will rise.

What can be done to control inflation?

Change interest rates

Every month the Bank of England decides whether to change interest rates or keep them the same. If the Bank believes inflation will increase, it raises interest rates. The cost of borrowing will increase so people will buy less.

Make sure there are enough staff

A shortage of trained people makes wages go up. One way of reducing inflation is to make sure that there are plenty of of people with the right skills. The government can provide training courses and help businesses train their staff.

Keep business costs down

In order to remain competitive, businesses will try to reduce their costs. They need to reduce their costs by keeping their payments for materials, land and staff as low as possible. They may need to reorganize so they are making their products as efficiently as possible. They will want to keep prices down to attract consumers.

If pensions don't increase at the same rate of inflation, pensioners can suffer

Key terms

economic growth: this happens when the country produces more goods and services from year to year

inflation: the general rise in prices

rate of inflation: the rate at which prices rise

Find out

What is the UK's current rate of inflation? Is this seen as good for the country? You might look at **www.treasury.gov.uk**.

Check your understanding

1 In your own words, explain what inflation is.

2 Name two things which can cause inflation. Explain why these things can lead to an increase in prices.

3 How might inflation affect someone who:

a is saving money?

b has a pension which is not linked to inflation?

c has trained in an area of work where there is a skills shortage, such as computer programming?

d is working in a business which is losing money and who doesn't have any specialist skills?

4 What can businesses do to help keep inflation rates down?

Making ends meet

Objective

Understand why people borrow money, and what can be done to prevent families and individuals from becoming excluded from the United Kingdom's economic system.

Getting you thinking

Borrowing

We took out an £80 000 mortgage. This is twice my partner's and my joint salaries. Our daughter has taken out a student loan to go to university. I took out a loan out to buy a new car. This summer we went to Florida using our credit cards.

I own four properties and rent the rooms to students. The rent, after taking away costs, gives me an income of £47 000 over the year. I also own shares in several companies and I earned £3000 from them this year. I earn £50 000 a year from my job. I'm going to take out another mortgage and buy another property.

1 What is the income of each person?

2 What do you understand by the term 'borrowing'?

3 Rank the people according to who you think earns the most to the least.

4 Who is finding it most it difficult to sort out their finances, and why?

My work is looking after my three children and making ends meet. I'm a single parent. The £100 I get from benefits doesn't cover my food and bills. I'm already behind in my rent and have had to borrow from the local moneylender. If I don't pay it back he will take my furniture. I've had to take on evening cleaning work, £20 a week, with my sister baby-sitting my children.

Spending or saving?

People use the money coming in each month to buy products and services.

If they haven't enough income they may decide to borrow or use their savings.

Able to save

Expenditure   Income

Use past savings or borrow money

Expenditure   Income

Is borrowing the solution?

If you want to borrow money, you must find someone to lend it. You will pay **interest** on the loan. This is an amount of money paid in addition to the amount borrowed. It is only safe to borrow money if you know you can pay it back.

People with low incomes and low skills will find it hard to borrow because it will be difficult for them to repay the loan. They may be below the **poverty line** and at risk of being economically excluded from society. This means that they don't have enough money to pay for the goods and services they need, such as housing, food and heating.

A quarter of Britain's population is living below the poverty line, and in more than one in six families nobody works. The poorest 20% earn 6.6% of all earnings compared with the 43% earned by the top 20% of earners.

Fairer shares

The government uses some of the money it raises from taxes to help the poor. It provides benefits, free health and education for all and subsidized housing. People who earn more pay more taxes. Poorer people receive more help. This is called **redistributing income**.

Providing real opportunities

The government doesn't want people to depend on benefits all the time. It wants them to be able to support themselves and become an active part of the economy. The government trains people in different skills and encourages them to seek work.

Working family tax credit means low earners can keep more of their income after tax

£200m of government money and £100m lottery money pays for neighbourhood nursery places so parents can work

More retraining opportunities

Minimum wage

? Why would a government want to spend money on the schemes shown in the newspaper headlines? How could these schemes help?

? Which schemes increase skills and which increase the rewards for working?

Check your understanding

1 Why do people borrow?

2 What does being economically excluded from society mean?

3 The government receives money from taxes. How does it use it to help the poor?

4 Why does the government run schemes to retrain people in new skills?

Discuss

1 Do you think it could be a problem for the *whole* of society if some people are economically excluded? Give reasons.

2 "Redistributing income is so unfair. I work hard for my money – why should I help pay for people who don't work?" How far do you agree or disagree with this statement? Give reasons.

Key terms

interest: extra payment paid to a lender by someone who has borrowed some money

poverty line: this is where incomes are considered to be below a level at which someone can afford to live

redistributing income: taking money from wealthier people through taxation, to give it to poorer people through benefits

Can the world be fairer?

Objective

Understand how difficult it is for some poor countries to develop.

Getting you thinking

	Niger	UK
How much the economy is worth per citizen	$190	$23 590
How fast the economy grew	−0.6% decline of $10 per person	2.1% increase of $495 per person
Number of people per doctor	35 140	667
How long people live	46 years	77 years
Number children dying before the age of 5 for every 1000 people	252	6
Personal computers per 1000 people	0.4	302.5
Adults who can read	15%	100%
International aid	Receives aid	Gives aid
Free education, healthcare and state pensions	No	Yes

World Development Report 1999

1 What evidence is there to suggest that the UK is better off than Niger?

2 What data might suggest the gap between the two countries is increasing?

3 Do you think the cost of buying basic needs is the same?

LEDCs and MEDCs

The world falls into two groups:

- The more economically developed (**MEDCs**), like the UK
- The less economically developed (**LEDCs**), like Niger and China.

This is a crude way of splitting the world into rich and poor countries. It masks different rates of economic growth and some countries do not fit into one group or another.

Debt: a cause of poverty?

Forty-one poor countries, 33 of them in Africa, owe about £150 billion in foreign debt. Every day the poorest countries of Sub-Saharan Africa pay £20 million to the West, whilst their economies decline, infant mortality rises and life expectancy falls.

To repay these debts, poor countries are forced to divert money away from healthcare, education and other vital services. Many children don't get the chance to go to school, mothers don't have prenatal care, and HIV-infected persons don't get the treatment they need.

People living in Niger. How does their standard of living compare to yours?

The beginnings of international debt

In the 1970s the world's richest nations lent huge sums of money to poorer countries. This money was sometimes lent to undemocratic corrupt governments. Much of it was spent on weapons, or wasted. It wasn't used to develop the country or help people living in poverty.

Many indebted countries, like Niger, are unable to escape the poverty trap because their economies have been growing at a slower rate than that of other countries. They are often dependent on selling one or two primary products, such as oil, bananas, uranium, copper or coffee. The prices they get for these have fallen. This means these countries will need to borrow more to maintain the same level of imports. When they borrow more, they get into greater debt.

Niger – a case study

Niger relies on selling uranium to richer countries who use it in their nuclear industries.

The nuclear industry needs less uranium so the value of Niger's exports are worth less.

Niger borrows money from international banks, other countries and international organizations to pay for imports such as food and other essential items.

Niger continues to borrow more money every year and gets into ever-greater debt. In 1999, the interest payment on the debt alone was $51 million.

Niger has to use its export earnings to pay interest on the debt, which now stands at over $1.1 billion.

? Why does Niger need to borrow money?

? What did it cost Niger to borrow the money in 1999?

? Do you think it will remain poor? Give reasons.

Cancelling the debt

Some debts have been cancelled as a result of campaigns like Jubilee 2000, and this has made a difference. In Uganda, twice as many children are now attending primary school. In Mozambique, they can now afford to vaccinate children against whooping cough, tetanus and diphtheria.

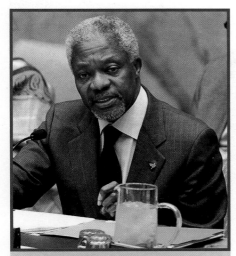

World leaders have promised to reduce global poverty by half by 2015. But Kofi Annan, Secretary General of the United Nations, says "Without debt cancellation, this target is a pipe dream."

Check your understanding

1 What are LEDCs and MEDCs?

2 Why can't indebted countries spend much money on vital services like health and education?

3 How did some governments damage their country's chances?

4 Give two reasons why it is difficult for the economies of LEDCs to grow.

5 Why would indebted countries be in a better situation if their debts were cancelled?

Find out

1 Find out more about world debt. Search for world debt on the internet or try the web addresses below:
www.oneworld.net
www.oxfam.org
www.dfid.gov.uk
www.worldbank.org (and go to the schools section)

2 Look for information about Jubilee 2000. What kind of organization is it? What are its aims? What campaigns have had success?

Key terms

LEDC: a less economically developed country

MEDC: a more economically developed country

Globalization

Getting you thinking

In an average week you will eat food from a dozen different countries; and in this way be linked to people all over the world. We depend on them to grow food – they depend on us to buy it.

1 List some advantages and disadvantages of this interdependence. Think about economic, social and environmental issues.

2 Do you think this interdependence means the world has become a 'smaller' place?

A shrinking world

Modern technology, combined with improved communication and transportation, has made it easier to trade around the world. Our nations are interdependent. It is not really the countries themselves that trade, but the businesses and consumers within those countries. The importance of trade is likely to increase with advances in technology. Already the internet allows us to buy from anywhere in the world.

Local economies, right down to the smallest local high streets, added together help make up a nation's economy. National economies added together make up the world economy.

The globalization game

Globalization has many players. Consumers, employees, large companies and nations all take part. There are winners and losers.

Consumer power:
If people don't like the price or quality they will buy from someone else. Businesses often try to produce as cheaply as possible.

Producer power:
Businesses can be very powerful. Many are very large. They can:

- force down the price they pay for resources because suppliers are frightened of losing their biggest customer
- keep wages down, because workers have few alternative jobs to go to
- fix prices higher if there is no competition
- fail to look after the environment if there are no laws to protect it.

Who is more powerful – big businesses or nations?

Economy of Republic of Ireland	$80 billion
Microsoft	$25.30 billion
Economy of Niger	$2 billion

The World Bank

Some companies' sales are bigger than many countries' economies. A country is stuck in one place: it can't move whereas a multinational company can produce wherever costs are lowest. Products, such as trainers, are often made in countries where labour is cheap. Businesses buy services from accounting to IT from countries around the world where labour is cheap. Many countries, however, welcome multinationals because they provide employment and skills. This helps the economy to grow.

Global branding

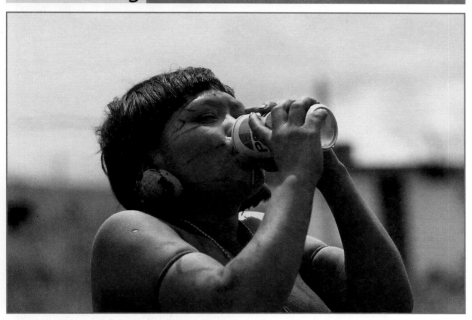

Some people are worried that global brands like McDonald's, Coca Cola, Pepsi, Nike and Gap erode the traditional culture of communities.

Can business be good?

More and more businesses are looking closely at their impact on the communities they serve. The Body Shop, The Coop Bank and Fairtrade organizations monitor their actions. Businesses are very aware of the damage that bad publicity can do. They run schemes to monitor their activities around the world. It is often difficult to carry this out and meet the standards set.

Discuss

"Global companies should not be allowed to employ people in LEDCs." Think of reasons for and against this statement.

Key terms

globalization: the increasing interdependence of the world

Check your understanding

1 In what ways might people think that producers have too much power?

2 It what situation might a supplier agree to sell goods to a buyer for a lower price?

3 If there is high unemployment in an area, why can companies pay lower wages?

4 Why do multinational companies produce their goods and services in different countries?

5 Explain why people might be worried about global brands.

Find out

1 Visit the Body Shop website at **www.bodyshop.co.uk** and find out about its trading charter.

2 Look up a newspaper page on the internet and search for articles about Nike, Coca Cola or McDonalds. Then visit the company's website. Try also to find websites which publish views against the company. Present your findings to the class.

Sweet shops and sweatshops

Getting you thinking

Chocolate: big business

Comic Relief helped a group of small farmers in Ghana, West Africa, to set up a company to trade their cocoa beans. As shareholders in the company, the farmers have a say in how their chocolate is produced and sold, and get a fair share of the profits. The farmers also ensure that employees who pick the beans are paid a fair wage.

In 1999 a US government investigation found that children as young as 11 were being sold into slavery to harvest cocoa beans in Ivory Coast. The US government wants chocolate manufacturers in the USA to label chocolate as 'Slave Free' if it has been made from cocoa from farms which do not exploit workers. The chocolate manufactures are trying to stop the government introducing this new law.

The average UK consumer spends about £60 a year on chocolate – and the total world market is worth £3.8 billion a year

1 Why did Comic Relief give money to the Ghanaian farmers?

2 Suggest one reason why the US chocolate manufacturers oppose the 'Slave Free' law.

3 Do you think the law will help the enslaved children in Ivory Coast? Give reasons.

Making trade fairer

Trade is a very important way for any country to earn money and create jobs. People and countries have traded for thousands of years, but in today's global economy, information, goods and money can be moved around the world at an incredible speed. Companies aim to make the best product at the cheapest price.

The World Trade Organization (WTO) is responsible for negotiating international trade agreements. Most rich countries want a **free trade** system in which the prices of goods are determined by the amount that people want to buy and sell. But many people believe such a system favours richer countries like USA and Japan and want the WTO to be reformed. They argue that world trade must be managed so the poorest countries benefit more. In other words, they want world trade to become 'fair trade'.

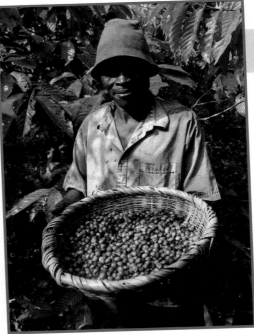

Is this farmer being paid a fair price?

Fair trade is trade that is good for the producer; a system that ensures more of the price consumers pay goes to the producer. Fair trade staff would be paid a fair wage, have good working conditions and be allowed to form trade unions to defend their rights.

Fair trade campaigns – such as the Clean Clothes Campaign (CCC) – have drawn attention to the working conditions of workers all around the world.

The Clean Clothes Code
for garment workers:

- Freedom to join a trade union
- No discrimination
- No forced or slave labour
- No workers under 15 years old
- Health and safety checks
- 48 hours maximum working week
- A fair wage.

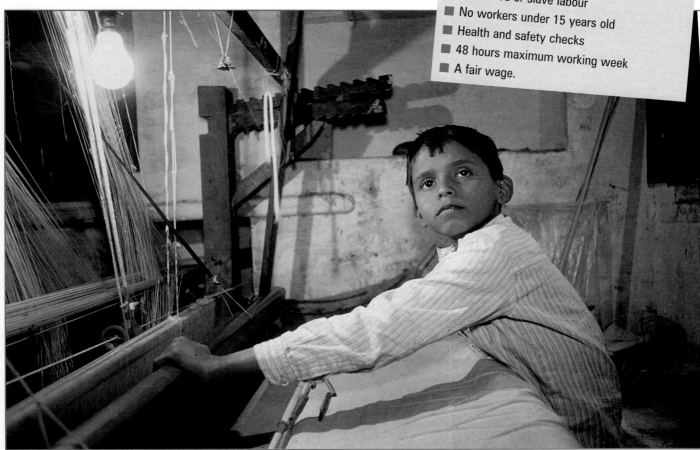

Check your understanding

1 In your own words, say what the World Trade Organization (WTO) does.

2 Why do some people want to reform the WTO?

3 How would 'fair trade' help workers in LEDCs?

4 What human rights do groups, such as the Clean Clothes Campaign, help to protect?

5 Do you think young people in the UK should boycott companies that sell 'dirty' clothes and trainers? Give reasons.

To buy or not to buy

The Clean Clothes Campaign does *not* believe consumers should **boycott** goods that are not 'clean' because it believes boycotts will put employees out of work. When the US government talked about bringing in a law to stop anything made by children under 15 from being imported in the USA, many child employeees in Bangladesh were thrown out of work and their families often went hungry as a result.

Find out

Use the internet to research UK companies trying to promote fair trade. Obtain details of company 'codes' – like the CCC code above – and use these to write an article on fair trade and it aims to help workers in LEDCs.

Key terms

boycott: to refuse to use or have anything to do with something

free trade: trade between countries which is not restricted by things like high taxes on imports

Worth a protest?

Getting you thinking

1 Think of some reasons why people might agree or disagree with this statement.

"Free trade is like putting the rabbit and the tiger in the same cage, the rabbit being the poor countries," claims a protestor.

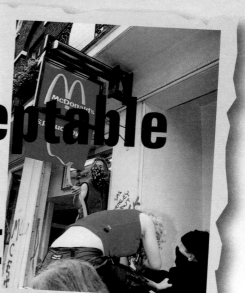

The unacceptable face of protest

Protest

Anti-globalization protests are a regular feature on the news. The protests are greatest when international organizations, like the International Monetary Fund (IMF) and World Trade Organization (WTO), meet to discuss free trade, poverty and wealth. The protestors are drawn from various pressure groups. This increases the number of protestors, but means their protests lack a clear aim. Some protestors are concerned with global warming, others with poverty, and still others worry about the impact of multinationals.

One such pressure group is the WDM (World Development Movement), which wants to change world trade rules. It is calling for strong international rules that put people's needs before free trade. It claims that money needed for clean water, health and education in poor countries is still being handed over to rich countries in debt repayments.

Receiving the right message

Your own views on an issue will be determined by what you hear. For some this will come from discussions with like-minded people. For most, the source will be the TV news or from their favourite newspaper. Whichever way, there is a danger that the information is biased. Biased information will favour one side or another, so it is always useful to hear both sides of the argument.

When the issue is global it can be more difficult to get your opinion across, because you have to influence powerful nations of world institutions. Again, pressure groups have a role to play in influencing opinion and providing an alternative view.

The work of international organizations

Three major international trade organizations are:

The World Trade Organization, which helps shape rules about trade so that it makes selling to other countries easier.

The World Bank, which provides loans to poorer countries for projects to help reduce poverty.

The International Monetary Fund, which promotes international financial cooperation and economic growth of international trade.

The anti-globalization movement says:	The international trade organizations say:
● International organizations, such as the IMF and World Bank, cause poverty because they encourage free trade which can damage LEDCs.	● Globalization and free trade is good for the poor. More international trade brings greater prosperity to the world and reduces poverty.
● The movement itself represents the poor, who have no voice themselves.	● Protest groups are undemocratic because they haven't been elected and so they cannot claim to represent people.
	● Protest groups are, in effect, preventing global efforts to tackle poverty.

How can pressure groups make their voices heard?

Pressure groups can lobby governments throughout the world and try to persuade them to their point of view. The groups can promote their case through publicity, including their internet sites, and they can protest.

Some recent protests have involved outbreaks of violence and damage to buildings. McDonald's is seen as a symbol of multinationals and is an easy target. Such actions by protestors, however few, are breaking the law. It gets media attention, but the protesters may lose the sympathy of the public.

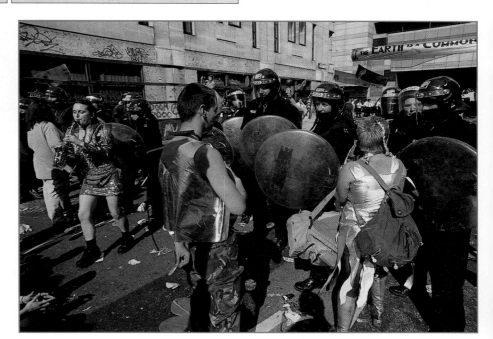

Find out

Look at the following websites for more information about globalization and prepare a short report on the arguments for and against increased globalization.
www.oneworld.net
www.worldbank.org
www.wto.org
www.oxfam.org.uk
www.dfid.gov.uk
www.imf.org

Discuss

The European Union has much higher import taxes on chocolate than cocoa beans. What effect does this have on the producers of cocoa beans?

Check your understanding

1 Why have different pressure groups joined together at certain world trade demonstrations? Make a list of the advantages and disadvantages of them doing so.

2 What other methods might pressure groups use to get their message across?

3 Why might pressure groups show bias when putting their case?

4 Might businesses and governments show bias too?

What is sustainable development?

Getting you thinking

Imagine you live in a very poor country, in a small rural village. You need fuel to cook food for your family. You may also need fuel to boil your drinking water to stop your children getting sick. The only way to get this fuel is to cut down the trees near your village. But you know that if you do this, the precious topsoil will blow away and eventually the desert will swallow up your village. What do you do?

1 What might happen if you don't boil your drinking water?

2 What are the long-term consequences if you cut down the trees for fuel?

3 Suggest possible solutions to this problem.

Hard choices

The villagers have to make the hard choice between solving a problem they have now and not making problems for the future. This kind of choice has to be made by everybody, although the circumstances are different everywhere.

In the UK and other MEDCs where there is economic growth, people expect their standard of living to improve. People can buy all sorts of things to make life more comfortable. They usually work shorter hours and have better access to healthcare and education.

These can all be good things but there are some drawbacks.

Growing food and building homes, roads, schools and hospitals uses land, energy and resources. The demand for products and services can mean pollution increases and natural resources are used up. In time these factors could actually decrease the standard of living. So the choice is between having what we want now or making sure future generations don't suffer.

> **?** List some of the land, energy and resources used in the following:
>
> - growing food
> - building motorways
> - foreign holidays.

Sustainable development

Sustainable development means we can improve the way people live today, without harming the prospects for the future. Different resources can be used so that scarce or dangerous materials are no longer needed. New materials can be designed to use less energy. Standards of living can be improved in ways which protect the environment, and harmful products can stop being made.

Values all people and all species

Protects the planet's water, air and soil

Sustainable development

Promotes local solutions to problems

Promotes and protects diversity

Protects the needs of future generations

Sustainable solutions

Energy

Because supplies of coal, oil and natural gas are limited they will only sustain our needs for so long before we will be forced to find alternative, sustainable sources of energy.

One solution could be wind power. There are already over 50 wind farms, mostly in Wales, Scotland and Cornwall. The amount of electricity generated by wind power in Europe rose by 30% in 1999. Offshore wind farms could, in theory, produce twice the UK's electricity requirements.

Food

For decades, large UK and European fishing fleets have fished in the North Sea. In recent years it has become clear that fish stocks there are so low there was a real danger that the North Sea would be fished out. Over-fishing had not allowed enough time for fish to breed and stocks to recover. Now fishing here is strictly controlled. Stocks are starting to recover and are a sustainable resource for the future.

Resources

Similarly, if you cut down forests for timber and paper faster than nature can replace them, you will end up with no trees.

However, trees are a **renewable resource**. Many countries now plant fast-growing trees to replace those chopped down. You now often see goods labelled: 'Made from timber from a sustainable forest'.

Check your understanding

1 In your own words, explain what is meant by 'sustainable development'.

2 Give one reason why it will be important in future to find sustainable solutions to environmental problems.

3 Why are the following considered to be sustainable developments?
- digging wells
- building schools
- planting trees

4 Can wind power be described as a sustainable energy source? Give reasons.

5 Why has commercial fishing in the North Sea been restricted?

A sustainable solution

Village Aid is a UK charity that works with people in the poorest regions of West Africa. All their projects aim to promote sustainable development. This is one project.

Every day, women from Janneh Kunda, a village in The Gambia, must walk from their homes to the rice fields. In the rainy season this can be dangerous. The bridges are old, unsafe and slippery with mud. The women have to carry tools, food for the day *and* their children. They must also carry the rice back home. The local people discussed these problems and decided they needed a safe bridge. It was built using the back end of an old lorry (which had been left for scrap), other local materials and local labour. It cost around £2000 – a tiny sum of money by western standards – and will last 25 years.

? Can the Janneh Kunda bridge be described as a sustainable solution to the women's problem? Give reasons.

Find out

Organizations such as Comic Relief, Oxfam, Christian Aid, Action Aid and many more, sponsor sustainable development projects. Research the work of one or more of these organizations and identify two to three problems they have addressed, and the solutions they and their local partners employed.

Key terms

renewable resource: able to be replaced or restored

sustainable development: living now in a way that doesn't damage the needs of future generations

Local solutions to global problems

Getting you thinking

Researchers from Sheffield University asked 2000 nine- to sixteen-year-olds from all around the country what they thought about their town centres. Most, but not all, described their home towns in negative terms. Here are some of the things they disliked.

The young people surveyed said they wanted more police, more security cameras and spaces where they could meet, where they would be safe and not be considered 'a nuisance' by adults.

1 Why did the young people want more security cameras?

2 "Kids today don't care about their neighbourhood. They mess everything up with graffiti and litter." Agree or disagree? Give reasons.

3 If you could talk to the architects who plan city centres, what improvements would you suggest?

Since 1992 local councils in UK have been working with local people on a wide range of projects. These are some of the long-term aims of these LA21 projects.

Reduce waste

Create nature reserves

Create safe routes to school

Create local employment

Reduce crime

Reduce racial harassment

Clean up streets and parks

Reduce pollution

Is Agenda 21 the answer?

At the United Nation's 'Earth Summit' in Rio de Janeiro in 1992, member countries agreed to work together to promote sustainable development around the world. **Local Agenda 21** (LA21) sets out how this is to be done at a local level. Although LA21 is a 'global' plan, it stresses the importance of involving local people when planning projects. They should be asked what *they* want for their local area. Local people often have valuable knowledge and experience, and are more likely to support a project if they feel they 'own' it. All LA21 projects should provide for the needs of the local community as a whole, and not exclude or discriminate against any group or minority.

Oldham, Lancashire

How people in Oldham think their community can be improved:

- ✓ Tackle street crime
- ✓ Improve street lighting
- ✓ More police on the beat
- ✓ More drugs education
- ✓ Improve health services
- ✓ Make people more aware of links between health and environment.

When the people of Oldham were asked about health as part of their LA21 plans, they didn't just comment on local hospitals and doctors. They also mentioned a wide range of social problems, including crime and violence, noisy and aggressive neighbours, drug abuse and pollution. Good health isn't just an absence of disease, they argued. Stress-related illness can be just as serious as physical illness such as heart disease.

Oxford

A local primary school uses a 'walking bus' to reduce car journeys to and from school. The walking bus, like an ordinary bus, has stops where parents wait to drop off and pick up their children, and a regular route and timetable. However, rather than use a motorized bus, everyone walks. Twenty to twenty-five children use the 'bus' every day.

Chicago USA

Rooftop gardens in the heart of Chicago will improve the air quality in the city because the plants absorb carbon dioxide and produce oxygen. The gardens will keep the sun's heat off the buildings, making them cooler and cut down the energy needed for air conditioning. The gardens also encourage birds to nest in the heart of the city.

Vaxjo, Sweden

Local people have voted to phase out the use of fossil fuels in all council buildings and transport. All new council buildings will be fitted with solar energy panels, and city buses will run on methane gas.

Check your understanding

1 In your own words, what is the *main* aim of Local Agenda 21?

2 Which of the LA21 aims do you think is the most important for your local area? Give reasons.

3 Pick two of the four LA21 projects above and say if they offer sustainable solutions. Give reasons.

Find out

Find out if your local council is promoting LA21 projects. For example, are they trying to reduce traffic congestion, pollution and noise? Are they introducing traffic calming schemes or trying to make streets safer for children and older residents?

Key terms

Local Agenda 21: a global plan to ask local people how they think their immediate environment could be improved

Waste not, want not

Objective

Understand local environmental problems associated with waste disposal, and some sustainable solutions.

Getting you thinking

"That polystyrene coffee cup you got from the vending machine, and are just about to bin, could be turned into a pencil. Thousands of acres of forest are felled every year to make pencils, but that doesn't have to happen," says inventor Edward Douglas-Miller of Remarkable Pencils, which produces 20 000 recycled plastic pens and pencils a day.

www.remarkable.com

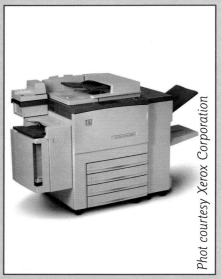

Phot courtesy Xerox Corporation

In Liverpool, CREATE employs people who are long-term unemployed to fix old electrical equipment for resale. They get paid and work towards an NVQ in engineering assembly. Many former trainees have found permanent jobs elsewhere.

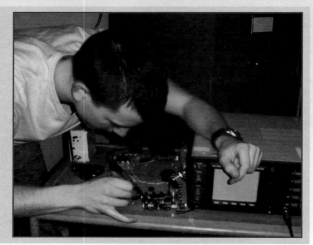

Xerox are now selling photocopiers with 'remanufactured' parts. The company takes back its own end-of-life photocopiers, and builds new machines out of reconditioned parts that are still in good condition. Reused and recycled parts can comprise up to 90% of a remanufactured machine's weight. Xerox estimates that it saves 200 million (US$) each year on purchases of new materials. The company designs its products with a 'waste-free' goal, aiming for all components to be reusable or recyclable.

Cash from trash

1 In what ways can the three projects in action above be described as 'environmentally friendly'?

2 Why do you think these projects were started?

3 Are these projects sustainable? Give reasons.

Getting rid of waste

Each person in the European Union produces 1 kg of household waste per day; which means a family of four produces 1 500 kg – more than the weight of a 5-door saloon car – every year.

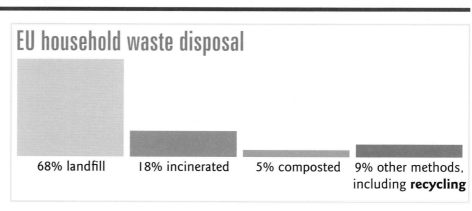

EU household waste disposal

68% landfill | 18% incinerated | 5% composted | 9% other methods, including **recycling**

Dump it?

Throwing rubbish into large holes is convenient but there are problems with this. Modern materials such as plastics do not rot and others can pollute the soil or groundwater. **Biodegradable** material, like kitchen and garden waste, produces methane gas – a **greenhouse gas** – when it decays (see page 124).

In 1995, all EU countries agreed to reduce the amount of biodegradable rubbish in landfill sites and set the following targets:

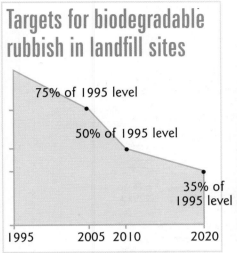

Targets for biodegradable rubbish in landfill sites

75% of 1995 level

50% of 1995 level

35% of 1995 level

1995   2005 2010   2020

Burn it?

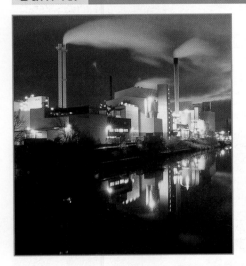

The UK government plans to incinerate more rubbish, but there are concerns about airborne pollution from incinerators. The latest incinerators are less polluting and more energy efficient than earlier types. But environmental groups opposed to incineration, such as Friends of the Earth, claim they still produce significant levels of dangerous chemicals, including dioxins. Many medical experts think there are links between dioxins and cancer. They believe that dioxins can affect children's growth, and even low levels are known to affect people's immune systems.

Recycle it?

There is some disagreement over how much waste can realistically be recycled. Friends of the Earth argue that 80% of all household waste could be recycled or composted. Germany, Netherlands and Switzerland already recycle 50% of household waste, compared to the UK's 9%.

The aim in the UK is to push recycling levels up to 60%. From an economic point of view, recycling is only viable if it costs less than using new materials, or if people want to pay the difference.

Find out

1 How could household waste by minimized? How could shops help with this problem?

2 How is household waste disposed of in your area? What plans do your council have to reduce the amount of biodegradable material they put into landfill sites?

3 If everyone composted their biodegradable waste, would this have a significant effect on how much rubbish would have to go into landfill sites? Give a reason.

4 Is recycling the only *safe* solution to waste disposal?

Check your understanding

1 Describe the advantages and disadvantages associated with using:
a) landfill sites and
b) incinerators.

2 Are landfill sites 'sustainable'? Give reasons.

Key terms

biodegradable: breaks down naturally through the action of bacteria

greenhouse gas: gases which trap the air around the Earth, causing a rise in temperature

recycle: to process products so they can be used again

Car crisis?

Getting you thinking

The European Union gives 50 million Euros to fund transport projects

Bristol:
A 'clean zone' in city centre. Reduced parking. Road pricing.

Graz (Austria):
Bus fleet and taxis converted to diesel. Polluting vehicles pay more to park.

Berlin:
State officials' cars and vans converted to natural gas. Can be used by private persons outside working hours, as part of a car-share scheme.

Rome:
City promotes electric scooters. On-street recharging facilities. Better traffic lights reduce congestion and pollution.

Sustainable transport

1 What is the aim of these projects?

2 Are these projects sustainable? Give reasons.

The real cost of motoring

A car gives you the freedom to go where you like, when you like. But what is the real cost of motoring?

Over 200 new cars are sold every hour in the UK, and though newer cars have 'greener' engines they still emit greenhouse gases. Road traffic is now a major cause of air pollution. Traffic fumes not only pollute our cities, they affect rural areas, too.

Government figures predict that road traffic will increase by 75% in the next 30 years. As congestion nears gridlock in many towns and cities, the average UK motorist spends a total of five days a year just sitting in traffic jams. Many people say they would use public transport if it were cheaper, cleaner and safer.

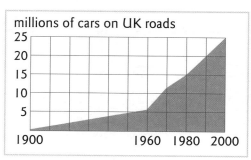

millions of cars on UK roads

Transport 2000

Possible solutions

Road pricing – how does it work?

Road users pay for using roads. Cars can be fitted with electronic number plates which give signals to special computers. The computer works out when the car was on a particular road and the driver is charged. In Singapore, this system has reduced rush-hour traffic, pollution and damge to roads. A drawback is that richer people can afford the charges, so poorer people could be disadvantaged.

Bike it!

The National Cycling Stategy in the UK aims to encourage people to cycle. The hope is to reduce pollution, improve local environments and people's health. Its work includes:

- providing more cycle routes so people can travel around easily and safely
- providing secure cycle parks at bus and train stations to make it convenient for people to use public transport for longer journeys
- encouraging train companies to provide spaces for bikes on trains.

Improving public transport

Better public transport might encourage people to stop using their cars so much. Possible plans:

- improve bus reliability
- decrease bus journey times
- reduce car traffic.

This could be done by:

- creating bus lanes on important routes and making sure cars don't use them
- giving priority at traffic lights to buses, pedestrians and cyclists
- stopping cars parking on busy routes.

Check your understanding

1 In what ways should public transport be improved to encourage more people to use it?

2 What are the advantages of the 'possible solutions'? Are there disadvantages?

Discuss

1 Is building more roads a *sustainable* solution to the UK's traffic problems? Give reasons.

2 There are now 20 million cars on UK roads, and this number is rising steadily. Do you think a law that limits car-ownership to one per family would be a good thing? Give reasons.

3 How does road traffic affect the lives of people in your local area? What could be done to improve the situation?

Find out

Research alternative forms of transport that might be used in towns and cities, such as electric-powered cars. Do they offer sustainable alternatives to petrol/diesel driven vehicles?

Key terms

road pricing: a scheme which charges road users according to how much they use a road

We all share the same air

Objective

Understand that all countries are interdependent with respect to pollution and global warming.

Getting you thinking

"Pollution doesn't need a passport"

After the Chernobyl nuclear power station fire in Russia in 1989, clouds of radioactive material were carried as far as the UK. In 2001, sheep on the Cumbrian fells were still being monitored for signs of radiation.

Chernobyl nuclear power station after the fire

The River Danube rises in Germany then flows through Austria, Hungary, Romania and Bulgaria before it reaches the Black Sea. So if pollution of the Danube is to be controlled effectively, then each of these countries has to be 'a good neighbour' to all the others.

1 Explain why pollution 'doesn't need a passport'.

2 What other ways can one country's action affect other countries' environment.

Climate change and global warming

Climate change is a complex subject and is not fully understood. Our climate is changing but scientists disagree about why it is happening and what the long-term effects of these global changes will be.

Many influential scientists believe the burning of **fossil fuels** is responsible for global warming. The concentration of carbon dioxide – CO_2, the main **greenhouse gas** – in the atmosphere is now at its highest for 400 000 years, and **global warming** is taking place faster than was expected. Temperatures are rising more quickly than at any time in the past 1000 years.

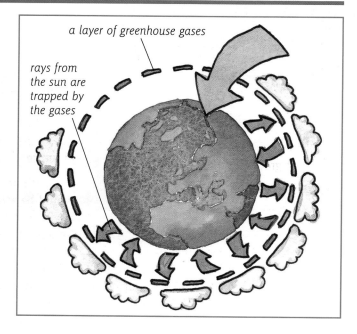

a layer of greenhouse gases

rays from the sun are trapped by the gases

What are the effects?

Climate changes can have both positive and negative effects. Higher levels of CO_2 in the atmosphere may improve crop yields, but they could also lead to water shortages.

There would be regional winners and losers from global warming. On balance, the LEDCs would suffer more than the MEDCs. There are already water shortages in countries such as Rwanda, Somalia and Kenya, and these are likely to get worse, bringing widespread crop failure and famine.

Rise in sea levels

As over half the world's population live on low-lying coastal plains and estuaries, millions of people could become environmental refugees.

In October 1999, over 10 000 people were washed away in floods in the Indian State of Orissa. Salt water ruined the crops and the land will take a long time to recover.

It might be necessary to increase pesticide and weedkiller use, which could lead to polluted rivers and lakes

Disease

Warmer and wetter conditions in other areas will increase waterborne infections like malaria, diarrhoea and dysentery. Higher temperatures would mean a rise in the number of pests, weeds and diseases.

Hurricanes, flooding and droughts

The possibility of more extreme weather threatens the livelihood of many of the poorest people in the world.

Richer nations, which produce the vast majority of greenhouse gases, will be affected by changes in weather patterns too. Violent storms and heavy rains to some areas and drought to others.

Cutting carbon: the Kyoto Protocol

In 1998, world leaders met in Kyoto, Japan, to discuss how to reduce global emissions of greenhouse gases. They agreed to reduce emissions by an average of 5% below 1990 levels by the year 2008. Many scientists argued this wasn't enough and that it would need emission cuts of up to 60%.

Check your understanding

1 In your own words, explain what greenhouse gases are.

2 List some of the likely effects of global warming.

3 Why do you think the world's leading climate scientists now argue that all nations must cooperate to reduce emissions of these gases?

Find out

1 Research the sources, both manufactured and natural, of greenhouse gas emissions. Use this information to suggest ways that emissions could be reduced in future.

2 Research which areas of the UK would be affected by rising sea levels. Which industries would be threatened by floods? How would local economies be affected? What, if anything, can government and/or local councils do to prepare for this?

Key terms

fossil fuel: a naturally-occurring fuel, such as coal or natural gas

global warming: the rise in average surface temperature of the Earth

---

The global village

The European family

Getting you thinking

The European Union (EU) is a trading area. When countries sell things to each other, they often have to pay taxes on products before they are allowed into the other country. The EU removed these taxes between countries within the EU so that they could trade freely with each other.

In order to allow this trade to be as free as possible, rules have been drawn up about a range of things that affect how businesses work. The rules aim to make competition fairer between countries so they are all working on 'a level playing field'.

1 Why do you think the European Union has rules like this?

2 If one country broke the rules, how might this affect other countries in the EU?

The rules are about: Protecting employees
Without EU regulations, one country could allow children to work in factories. It could make things more cheaply because wages would be lower.

Protecting the environment
If one country allowed businesses to pollute the environment, production would be cheaper because they wouldn't have to clean up the mess that was made.

Guaranteeing product standards
If a country is making poor-quality products, they may be dangerous.

Promoting fair competition
Businesses are not allowed to have too much power. For example, if a business controlled prices unfairly this would hurt the customer.

What is the European Union?

At the end of World War II in 1945, the countries of Europe were anxious that war should not break out again. By joining together more closely, it was felt that war would be less likely. Ever since 1958, more countries have become involved and have worked together ever closer in all sorts of areas, including economics, politics, the environment and social issues.

Sweden
Netherlands
Finland
UK
Ireland
Denmark
Germany
Belgium
Austria
Luxembourg
France
Portugal   Spain   Italy   Greece

The European Union:

- promotes economic and social progress
- gives the EU a voice on the international scene
- introduces EU citizenship
- develops an area of freedom, security and justice
- maintains and establishes EU regulations.

KEY

Countries which are currently members of the EU

Countries which are likely to become members by 2004

Countries which would like to become members

How the EU works

All member countries, or **Member States**, of the EU elect Members of the European Parliament (MEPs). MEPs have much bigger constituencies than MPs in each country because the European Parliament has to represent all the member countries – 370 million people in total. The European Parliament has 626 members altogether. The UK Parliament has 659 MPs compared with 87 MEPs.

The Parliament is one of the five organizations that run the EU. It is, however, not quite like the UK Parliament, which has power to make laws. Look at the diagram below to decide where the power lies.

Where does the power lie?

The Council of Ministers

- Main decision-making body
- Made up of one minister from each member state
- Discusses proposals for new regulations put forward by the European Commission.

The European Commission

- Proposes new regulations
- Makes sure EU regulations are carried out and oversees the EU administration.

The European Parliament

- Discusses proposals for regulations put forward by the European Commission
- Enforces EU regulations
- Can call for new policies to be launched and for existing ones to be changed.

The Court of Auditors

- Checks that EU money has been spent properly.

The Court of Justice

- Decides whether European regulations have been broken.

Check your understanding

1 Which organization in the EU holds most power?

2 How is the EU different from the UK in this respect?

Find out

1 Which European constituency are you in?

2 Who is your MEP?

3 Which political party do they represent?

Discuss

How democratic is decision-making in the EU compared with the UK?

Key terms

Member State: countries which are members of the EU

A family member?

Objectives

Understand that business and citizenship in the UK is affected by European Union regulations.

Getting you thinking

A bigger market

Herman Miller is an international business based in the USA. However, it makes office furniture in the UK, Germany and Italy and sells it throughout Europe. There is a lot of competition between businesses selling office furniture so Herman Miller must keep its prices low and look after its customers. Being in the EU means that there are fewer forms to fill in and fewer delays when lorries cross the borders between European countries. There are also no taxes to pay when furniture is sold to other European countries. If it came from the USA, for example, there would be taxes to pay.

Because the goods are manufactured in the EU, it means that both the materials that they need to make the furniture and the finished products can be delivered more quickly, reliably and cheaply.

1. Do you think that Herman Miller thinks the EU is a good or bad thing?

2. Why do you think Herman Miller wants to keep factories going in Europe?

3. How does the EU affect customers?

Inside or out?

The EU combines its member states into one big market. Businesses can sell their products in any EU state so there is lots of competition. This means that prices should be lower.

The downside is that things bought from countries outside the EU are more expensive. A tax, or **customs duty**, has to be paid on goods from other parts of the world, so these goods would probably cost more for an EU consumer.

These factors have meant that the UK buys and sells more products to EU countries than any other part of the world.

What about the Euro?

The **Euro** was set up on 1 January 1999. It is the **single currency** for members of the EU.

When the Euro was launched, the UK decided not to join because, among other things, the economy was not in line with other European countries.

The Euro can make things more straightforward.

- People and businesses don't have to change money from one currency to another. This makes things cheaper because banks charge for changing money.

- It makes things more certain. The value of currencies change against each other. If you go on holiday to the USA, the number of dollars you can buy with your pounds will change from day to day. If everyone in Europe uses the Euro, a business knows that there will be no change in the price it receives for products sold in other European Union countries.

Not everyone is in favour of the Euro. The main concern is that it reduces a country's control over its own economy. If a lot of people are unemployed, the government might want to use policies that help to create jobs. This might be difficult if it did not fit with EU policy.

Citizens of the European Union

Any citizen of a country within the EU is automatically an EU citizen. This does not interfere with your national rights but adds four special rights to them:

- **_Freedom to move and take up residence anywhere in the Union_**
  You can get a job anywhere in the EU. It is much harder to get work in other parts of the world.
- **_The right to vote and stand in local government and European Parliament elections in the country of residence_**
  A British citizen living in another Member State could stand for election there.
- **_Representatives of any Member State will offer protection to EU citizens in countries where an individual's country is not represented_**
  Wherever you are in the world, an EU representative can help you out if you are in difficulties.
- **_The right of appeal to the European ombudsman_**
  If you feel that EU rulings have not been carried out properly, you can appeal to the ombudsman to investigate.

---

europa

ES
DA
DE
EL
► EN ◄
FR
IT
NL
PT
FI
SV

News

Abc

Institutions

Policies

Citizens rights

The European Union's prime concern is to place individuals and their interests at the heart of European integration. The European institutions regard respect for fundamental rights as a general principle of European law and have developed legislation on freedom of movement within the European Union.

With the Treaty of Maastricht, the link between the citizens in the Member States and the European Union became more direct, with the creation of the concept of European citizenship, which introduced a series of civil and political rights. These rights were further developed by the Treaty of Amsterdam, which also specified the link between national citizenship and European citizenship

Further information on:

★ **fundamental rights**

★ **rights relating to freedom of movement within the European Union**

★ **rights relating to European citizenship**

| ★ Key issues | @ Mail-box | ! What's new? | ? Search | ⓘ Information |

www.europa.eu.int

Check your understanding

1 Give two reasons why it can be cheaper to buy goods from within the European Union than from outside it.

2 Why could belonging to the Euro be a problem for individual EU countries?

3 As a British citizen, would you be allowed to work in Spain? Give reasons.

4 If you were travelling outside the European Union and you needed help from officials, who could you go to if you found out there was no British embassy or representative in that area?

Find out

1 Is there a plan for the United Kingdom to join the Euro? If so, what is happening? If not, what are the issues? If the process is underway, what stage has it reached?

2 Collect as much information about the Euro as possible. Make a display, using the evidence you have collected, about how the Euro is affecting the UK.

3 What does European citizenship mean to people who you know? Would they describe themselves as Europeans? Are there any situations when they would be more or less likely to call themselves Europeans?

Key terms

customs duty: taxes on products bought from other countries

Euro: the name of the single currency used by a group of countries within the European Union (Belgium, Germany, Spain, France, Ireland, Italy, Luxembourg, the Netherlands, Austria, Portugal and Finland)

European ombudsman: a person who investigates complaints against the EU

single currency: this is the Euro, so called as it is used in most of the EU Member States

---

The Commonwealth

Objective

Understand how the Commonwealth has changed from its origins, and the type of work it does today.

Getting you thinking

Daily bread

Elizabeth Namwala, 29, is a mother living in Chipata Compound, a low-income housing estate in Lusaka, Zambia. Elizabeth used to sell four to five pans of bread a day.

She then received some loans from the Commonwealth Youth Credit Initiative. The money went towards buying stocks of ingredients. Now, Elizabeth sells 50 pans of bread a day. She repaid her first and second loans before the due date and is now repaying a third. Elizabeth has expanded her business and employs five young people. She has improved her house, and her living standards have risen.

1 Who gave Elizabeth her loan?

2 How did the loan help Elizabeth?

3 How did the loan help other people?

4 Why do you think the Commonwealth Youth Credit Initiative gives loans to people in developing countries?

The Commonwealth today

The **Commonwealth of Nations**, usually just called the Commonwealth, is an association of countries, most of which are or were ruled by Britain. However, today's Commonwealth is a world away from the handful of countries which were the first members. From Africa to Asia, from the Pacific to the Caribbean, the Commonwealth's 1.7 billion people make up 30% of the world's population.

The modern Commonwealth helps to advance democracy, human rights, and sustainable economic and social development within its member countries and beyond. All the countries have English as a common working language and similar systems of law, public administration and education. The Commonwealth has built on its shared history to become a vibrant and growing association of states.

Commonwealth members

- **As a force for making democracy work**
  The Commonwealth helps its members to develop working democracy. It sends observers to check that elections are carried out properly.

- **As a platform for building global agreement**
  It holds conferences which bring all the countries together to discuss major issues. This help everyone to work together better.

- **As a source of practical help for sustainable development**
  The Commonwealth helps people to work so they can look after themselves, and has programmes which aim to look after the environment.

How does it do its work?

The Commonwealth has all sorts of ways of helping people and encouraging them to work together. Here are two examples:

The Commonwealth Fund for Technical Cooperation (CFTC)

The CFTC promotes economic and social development, and helps to overcome poverty in member countries. The skills of member countries are used to help others. Advisors go to other countries to help in agriculture, enterprise, trade, legal issues, etc.

The Commonwealth Youth Credit Initiative (CYCI)

The CYCI is a small enterprise scheme for young people providing 'micro-credit' (small-scale lending), training and enterprise development. Low-cost, easily accessible credit and training can bring economic self-sufficiency to the poorest young people. CYCI provides these services using the following methods:

- low interest rates
- low training costs
- use of young people to support each other, and to encourage saving and the paying back of loans
- ongoing training and monitoring of enterprises.

Check your understanding

1 What are the origins of the Commonwealth?

2 How has it changes over the years?

3 What is its mission today?

4 Describe some ways in which it achieves its mission?

Find out

1 Have any countries joined the Commonwealth recently?

2 What are the conditions for joining the Commonwealth?

3 Why do countries want to be members of the Commonwealth?

4 Find an example of a recent Commonwealth sustainable development programme and present your findings to the class.

Key terms

Commonwealth of Nations: a voluntary group of 54 independent countries

---

The global village

A united world?

Objective

Understand the work of the United Nations and consider its role in the world.

Getting you thinking

For generations, Kosovo has been fought over by Serbs and Albanians. Both peoples have centuries' old claims to the land.

Throughout the 1990s, Serbs and Albanians were at war with each other over control of the region. Then, in July 1999, the **United Nations** stepped in to keep the peace. UN personnel dealt with law and order, health and education, and ensuring the safe return of **refugees** to their homes.

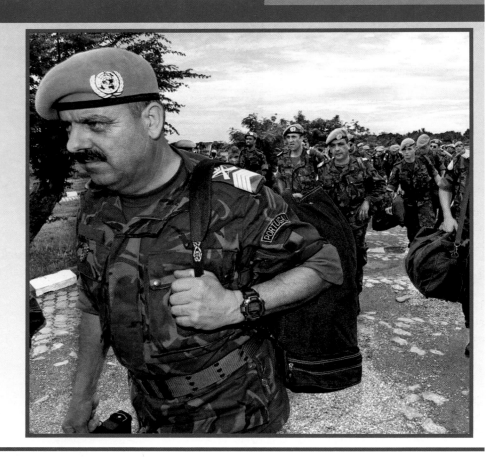

1 Why do you think the Serbs and Albanians needed help to bring the war to an end? What might have happened if it hadn't?

2 Why do you think refugees needed help to find their families and return home?

3 Why do you think people respect the soldiers from the UN?

The United Nations (UN)

Nearly every nation in the world belongs to the UN. Its membership in 2002 totalled 189 countries.

When states join, they agree to accept the UN charter. The aims of the charter are:

● to maintain international peace and security

● to develop friendly relations among nations

● to cooperate in solving international problems and in promoting respect for human rights

● to be a centre for harmonizing the actions of nations.

The United Nations is not a world government and it does not make laws. It does, however, help to resolve international conflict and makes policies on matters affecting us all. At the UN, all the Member States have a voice and can vote in this process.

Peacekeeping – the work of the UN Security Council

The Security Council is made up of five permanent members – including the United Kingdom – and 15 non-permanent members who are elected for two years at a time. As the world changes, the number of permanent members may change.

The Security Council:

● can investigate any international dispute

● recommend ways of reaching a settlement

● is responsible for peacekeeping forces.

Refugees

For more than five decades the United Nations High Commission on Refugees has been helping the world's uprooted peoples.

The agency's first task was to help an estimated one million people after World War II. During the 1950s the refugee crisis spread to Africa, Asia and then back to Europe. It had become a global problem.

During its lifetime the agency has assisted an estimated 50 million refugees to restart their lives.

An Afghan family enters Pakistan from Afghanistan to go to a refugee camp. February 2002.

Development and trade

The UN also aims to help developing countries grow and trade fairly with the rest of the world. It works to improve the standard of living by making recommendations and giving guidance on economic development.

Humanitarian action and human rights

Child soldiers in Africa are looked after by the UN and educated in order to help them to fit into society again. Often their families can't be found. This is just one of many projects to help people in difficulties.

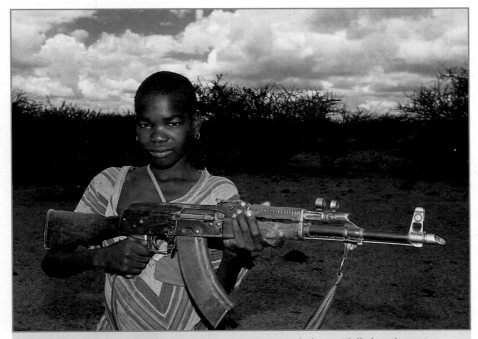

"The soldiers gave me training. They gave me a gun. I took drugs. I killed civilians. Lots. It was just war, what I did then. I only took orders. I knew it was bad. It was not my wish."

Check your understanding

1 What kind of work does the UN do?

2 Is the UN a government? Explain your answer.

3 Describe the Security Council's responsibilities.

4 Why is the UK important in the Security Council?

5 Why do you think the UN needs to intervene in the conflicts mentioned?

6 Why might the UN be able to help refugees more effectively than individual countries?

7 Which human rights are being denied the child soldiers?

Find out

1 Research a current UN peacekeeping operation. Why are people fighting? How is the UN helping? Is it 'maintaining international peace and security'?

2 Find a recent example of work done by the UN High Commission on Refugees. Why had the refugees left home? How has the High Commission helped?

Key terms

refugees: people who have been forced to leave their country and must live somewhere else

United Nations: an international organization that tries to encourage peace, cooperation and friendship between countries

Global crisis – global action

Objective

Understand the impact of HIV/AIDS and the work the United Nations does to combat this epidemic.

Getting you thinking

HIV/AIDS: a global problem

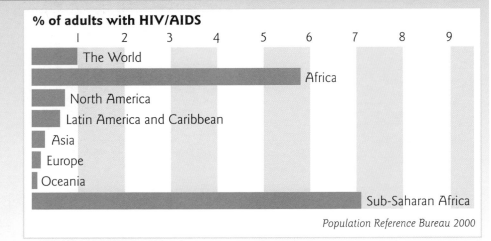

% of adults with HIV/AIDS

- The World
- Africa
- North America
- Latin America and Caribbean
- Asia
- Europe
- Oceania
- Sub-Saharan Africa

Population Reference Bureau 2000

1 Which continent has the highest rates of **HIV/AIDS**?

2 Suggest reasons for the difference between infection rates in Europe and sub-Saharan Africa

Researched image of AIDS sufferers in Sub-Saharan Africa

Dying of ignorance

In the year 2000, the number of 10- to 19-year-olds on the planet reached one billion. Most of these young people live in LEDCs.

Half of all new HIV infection is occurring in young people. Because of a lack of even basic health education, many young people in LEDCs are unaware of the risks they face and don't know how to protect themselves. Poor countries can't afford to set up clinics, provide HIV testing or distribute free condoms.

UNICEF – an agency of the UN – estimates that one-half of today's 15-year-olds in Botswana and South Africa will die from AIDS.

UNAIDS – the UN and the World Health Organization at work

The United Nations works with many other organizations worldwide to fight the spread of HIV/AIDS. In 1987 it set up a special global programme to deal with the problem. Since 1996 this programme has been run by UNAIDS, with the help of 30 other UN organisations, such as the World Health Organization (WHO) and UNICEF.

UNAIDS' role is to help governments to help themselves, and not to impose a 'UN solution' on a local problem.

Here are some examples of projects that have been supported by UNAIDS.

- UNAIDS teamed up with MTV to promote HIV/AIDS awareness to its one billion viewers around the world.
- UNAIDS worked with the Ministry of Health in Brazil on a project which targeted 100 000 'at-risk' teenagers and 80 000 injecting drug users.
- UNAIDS sponsored the TV soap, *I Need to Know*, which goes out on 20 television stations across Nigeria. The programme tries to persuade viewers that 'silence can be deadly', and encourages young people to speak out about taboo topics like HIV/AIDS.
- UNAIDS works with local agencies in southern Africa on a project aimed at preventing HIV/AIDS infection, particularly in adolescent girls.
- UNAIDS collaborates with local churches in Chikankata, Zambia, helping to care for 1500 'AIDS orphans' from local villages.

? Why did UNAIDS team up with MTV?

? Why did the Brazilian government target teenagers and injecting drug users? What other groups might have been targeted?

? Give reasons why UNAIDS used a TV soap to get health messages across in Nigeria.

? Why does UNAIDS think it is important to support local programmes?

Wake up to HIV/AIDS

Kindlimuka is Mozambique's first self-help group for people living with HIV/AIDS. UNICEF supports the group.

Over 20 million people in Mozambique are HIV positive, with some 600 new infections every day. Of the new infections, 45% of new sufferers are under the age of 25. Most do not know they are infected.

Kindlimuka, which means 'wake up', works with local schoolchildren. The director, Adriano Matsinhe, says, "Because I look healthy, the children think I'm paid to say I'm HIV-positive."

Matsinhe is one of the few people in Mozambique who has openly admitted he is HIV-positive on television. The stigma of HIV/AIDS is one of the greatest challenges sufferers have to face, and Kindlimuka has been a breakthrough. It's a real community service. Many families now visit the centre.

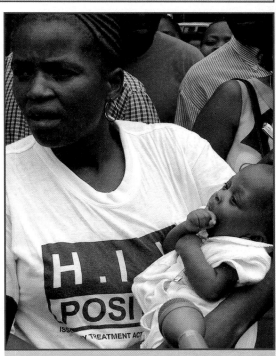

A South African mother carrying her four-month-old HIV-positive baby.

Check your understanding

1 Why are so many young people in LEDCs 'dying of ignorance'?

2 HIV/AIDS is a global problem, but why is it a more urgent problem in Africa than in Europe?

3 Why do you think the Mozambique project is called 'wake up'?

4 In your own words, what is the main challenge faced by AIDS workers such as Adriano?

Discuss

HIV/AIDS will have long-term economic effects in LEDCs, such as Mozambique. In groups, discuss how the epidemic might affect the following in a poor country:

- family earnings
- education levels
- food supplies
- health services.

Find out

Research, via organisations such as the Terence Higgins Trust, rates of HIV infection in the UK and the support available to those infected. Compare UK rates and support with information for another region.

Key terms

AIDS: Acquired Immune Deficiency Syndrome – a disease which destroys people's natural defences against diseases

HIV: Human Immunodeficiency Virus – a virus that reduces people's resistance to illness and can cause AIDS

A louder voice

Objective

Understand how individuals can work with international organizations to help bring about change in the world.

Getting you thinking

1 Why are people tortured?

2 How many countries use torture?

3 Why is it wrong?

4 How do you think you can help Amnesty International to end torture?

TORTURE is wrong, unjust and illegal.
It should never happen to anyone.

EVERYONE has the right not to be tortured. Everyone also has the right to be free of the threat of torture. But in the world in which we live, many people are tortured. In fact, in more than 150 countries torture is used to hurt, frighten and punish people.

This booklet is about torture and what you can do to stop torture. It has been written by an organization called Amnesty International.

Please help us to make the world free of torture.

Stop Torture

Why Amnesty?

Amnesty International is a worldwide pressure group that campaigns to save people who are imprisoned, hurt or threatened by the government of a country. It promotes the values of the Universal Declaration of Human Rights.

How does Amnesty International work?

Amnesty International has around one million members and supporters in 162 countries. Activities range from public demonstrations to letter writing, from human rights education to fundraising concerts, from individual appeals on a particular case to global campaigns on a particular issue.

Amnesty International is impartial and independent of any government or religion.

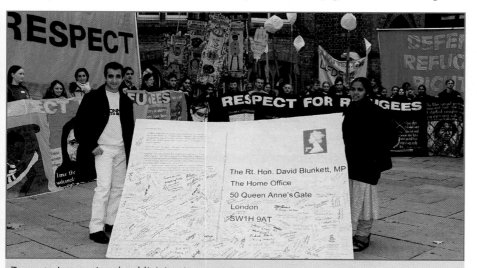

Amnesty International publicizing its campaign

Armenia
Conscientious objector

Amnesty International has learned that Rafik Tonoian was released on 21 May 2001 after having served one third of his sentence ... The authorities received over 1000 appeals ...

Karen Yegoian, the other conscientious objector, is still in prison.

Please continue appeals on his behalf.

An Amnesty update on a past campaign and an appeal to its members to keep writing to save another prisoner of conscience

Campaigning

Amnesty, like many other pressure groups, is run by its members. Its aim is to put pressure on governments and other organizations to change the way they behave. By joining together, people can have a greater effect.

What can be done?

Pressure groups work in many different ways. For example, Greenpeace often encourages people to send a message. It supplies e-cards that can be emailed to anyone.

It also campaigns in other ways:

- it has ships which are sent to places where the environment is under threat
- they have anchored where a country was carrying out nuclear tests
- they have boarded an oil platform which was to be sunk with the threat of pollution.

Their actions are sometimes outside the law, but they feel very strongly that these methods are the most effective way of getting people to take notice.

A letter on the Greenpeace website

Source: Greenpeace

> I work for a big company and I have to tell you that Greenpeace's tactics do make an impression and have impact. In this age of 'spin' and image consciousness, the last thing most companies want is visible, messy, physical confrontation. The mere existence of Greenpeace (and other activist groups) and the threat of embarrassing media coverage puts a check on bad corporate behaviour. Even if they deny this, it is always in the back of their mind. Your work – and especially your high profile activities – help us keep the business people from getting completely out of control.
>
> So, don't change, don't become more mainstream, don't smooth off the rough edges, and don't dumb-down to mediocrity. Insiders like me need your visibility and activism!!

Amnesty uses the power of the individual to put on the pressure. The organization publicizes human rights abuses and asks its members to write to the relevant governments or authorities in protest. One letter would have little effect but hundreds or thousands might make people listen. These are the sorts of strategies used by many large pressure groups.

Greenpeace activists boarding an oil platform to prevent it being sunk

Check your understanding

1 What is the main focus of Amnesty International's work?

2 How can individuals join in Amnesty International's campaigns?

3 Why is group pressure more effective than individual pressure?

4 Describe the effect Greenpeace can have on large corporations.

Action

1 Is there an Amnesty International or Greenpeace local action group in your area? Interview members of the group and find out what they do.

2 Choose an international pressure group and find out how it works. What are its successes? How did they happen? Present your findings to the class.

Key terms

pressure group: a group of people who try to change public opinion or government policy to their own views or beliefs

Glossary

accountable: if you are accountable for something, you are responsible for it and have to explain your actions

Act: a law passed by government

AIDS: acquired immune deficiency syndrome – a disease which destroys people's natural defences against diseases

appeal: a request for a decision made by a court to reviewed

Assembly: a body of elected people to decide on some areas of spending in a region

bias: to favour one thing over another unfairly

bill: a proposal to change something in law

biodegradable: breaks down naturally through the action of bacteria

boycott: to refuse to use or have anything to do with something

British national: citizens or subjects of the United Kingdom

budget: this happens every year. The Chancellor of the Exchequer explains how the government will raise and spend its money

business rates: a form of tax paid by all the businesses in an area. The amount a business pays depends on the rent that could be charged for their premises

cabinet: the main decision-making body of the council

cabinet [the government's]: a group of MPs who head major government departments. It meets weekly to make decisions about how government policy will be carried out

canvassing: the process by which people go round and try to persuade voters to vote for their party in an election

censorship: limiting the information given to the general public

Chancellor of the Exchequer: the member of the government who is responsible for the country's finances

Chief Executive: an employee of the council, responsible for the smooth running of services

Citizens Advice Bureau: (CAB): an organization that offers free advice on consumer and other legal matters

civil law: this covers disputes between individuals or groups. Civil law cases are often about rights

Commonwealth of Nations: a voluntary group of 54 independent countries

community: a group of people in close contact and who share common interests and values

community sentence: when someone who has been convicted of a crime, works in the community (clearing litter, for example) rather than going to prison

compensation: making amends for something; something given to make good a loss

constituency: the area represented by an MP

consumer: a person who buys goods or services for their own needs

contract of employment: a document which details an employee's and employer's responsibilities for a particular job

Convention: an agreement (often between governments)

council: a group of people who are elected to look after the affairs of a town, district or county

councillor: a member of a local council, elected by people in that area

council tax: a tax paid by everyone who lives in an area. It is based on the value of their house

county court: a local court that has limited powers in civil cases (laws operating between people)

criminal law: this deals with offences such as murder and drug dealing. These cases are between the Crown Prosecution Service (acting for all citizens) and the offender

crown court: courts held in towns in England and Wales where judges hear cases

cultural diversity: the range of different groups that make up a wider population

customs duty: taxes on products bought from other countries

Data Protection Act: this Act limits the way that information that is stored on computers can be used

Declaration: a document setting down aims and intentions

devolution: the transfer of power from central government to regional government

dioxin: chemical by-products from the manufacture of some herbicides

discrimination (racial, sex and disability): when a person is treated less favourably because of their colour, ethnic origins, gender or disability

dismissal: when employers end an employee's contract of employment (sometimes called 'sacking')

division of labour: where employees concentrate on a particular task or job at which they are expert

dual heritage: people with parents or ancestors of different origins

economic growth: this happens when the country produces more goods and services from year to year

economy: this is made up of all the organizations that provide goods and services, and all the individuals and organizations that buy them

editor: the person who is responsible for the content of a newspaper or television or radio programme

election: selection of one or more people for an official position by voting (in the UK, almost everyone over 18 can vote)

emigration: leaving your homeland to live in another country

employment laws: passed by Parliament and the European Union that set out the rights and responsibilities of employers and employees

Euro: the name of the single currency used by a group of countries within the European Union (Belgium, Germany, Spain, France, Ireland, Italy, Luxembourg, the Netherlands, Austria, Portugal and Finland)

European ombudsman: a person who investigates complaints against the EU

first past the post: an electoral system where voters have one vote per constituency and the candidate with the most votes wins

Forward Plan: a document which sets out the aims of the council in the long term

fossil fuel: a naturally-occurring fuel, such as coal or natural gas

Freedom of Information Act: a law which gives open access to information about individuals, business and government

free trade: trade between countries which is not restricted by things like high taxes on imports

general election: an election for a new government. In the UK, these take place at least every five years

globalization: the increasing interdependence of the world

global warming: the rise in average surface temperature of the Earth

government revenue: the money raised by the government

greenhouse gas: gases which trap the air around the Earth, causing a rise in temperature

Green Paper: this puts forward ideas that the government wants discussed before it starts to develop a policy

hereditary peers: people who inherited the title 'Lord'

High Court: the highest court where judges hear cases on serious crimes

HIV: human immunodeficiency virus – a virus that reduces people's resistance to illness and can cause AIDS

homophobic: fear or hatred of homosexuals

House of Commons: the more powerful of the two parts of the British Parliament. Its members are elected by the public

human rights: something people are morally or legally allowed to do or have

identity: who or what something is

identity card: a card that establishes someone's identity

immigration: moving to another country to live there

inclusive education: schooling that involves everyone, regardless of disability or non-disability

industrial tribunal: a court dealing only with disagreements over employment laws

inflation: the general rise in prices

interdependent: where businesses need each other to survive

interest: extra payment paid to a lender by someone who has borrowed some money

journalist: a person who gathers news and produces reports for the media

judge: a person who decides questions of law in a court

judiciary: all the judges in a country

jury: a group of people who decide if someone is guilty in a court of law

LEDC: a less economically developed country

legal right: a right which is protected by law

libel: writing incorrect things about people

lobby: to try to persuade MPs to support a particular point of view. This used to happen in the 'lobby', or hallway, on the way into Parliament

Local Agenda 21: a global plan to ask local people how they think their immediate environment could be improved

magistrate: a public officer who deals with civil cases

magistrates' court: a court held before two or more public officers dealing with minor crimes

majority: the party with a majority has won a bigger proportion of the votes than the others

manifesto: a published statement of the aims and policies of a political party

mayor: a member of the council who is selected to be its representative on ceremonial occasions. In some areas they are the elected leader

MEDC: a more economically developed country

media: ways of communicating with large numbers of people

Member of Parliament: a person who has been elected to represent a constituency in parliament

Member State: countries which are members of the EU

Minister of State: an assistant to the Secretary of State

minority: a small part of a larger group of people

minutes: a formal record of what has been said at a meeting

mitigating: making something less intense or severe

multicultural community: a community made up of people from many different cultural or ethnic groups

neighbourhood: a local area within which people live as neighbours, sharing living space and interests

ombudsman: a person who investigates complaints against the government or a public organization

opinion poll: questioning a sample of the population to build a picture of the views of the public on a particular topic

opposition: political parties who are not in power

people's peers: people who are selected to sit in the House of Lords

political party: organized groups of people with common aims who put up candidates up for elections

polling station: a place where votes are cast – often a school, library or village hall

postal voting: voters can make their vote by post, rather than by going to a polling station

poverty line: this is where incomes are considered to be below a level at which someone can afford to live

Press Code: guidelines for the media and journalists about the information they gather and how they gather it

pressure group: a group of people who try to change public opinion or government policy to their own views or beliefs

Prime Minister the leader of the majority party in the House of Commons and the leader of the government

private sector: this section of the economy is made up of businesses or organizations that are owned by individuals or by shareholders

profit: the money that you gain when you sell something for more than you paid for it or than it cost to make

proportional representation: an electoral system in which the number of seats a party wins is roughly proportional to its national share of the vote

public sector: this is made up of organizations owned or run by the government and local councils

racism: the idea that some people of different origins are not as good as others

rate of inflation: the rate at which prices rise

recorder: a barrister of solicitor of at least 10 years experience who acts as a part-time judge in a crown court

recycle: to process products so they can be used again

redistributing income: taking money from wealthier people through taxation, to give it to poorer people through benefits

redundancy: when a person loses their job because the job doesn't need to be done anymore

redundant: this means you lost your job because the job has ceased to exist

referendum: a vote by the whole electorate on a particular issue

refugees: people who have been forced to leave their country and must live somewhere else

rehabilitation: restoring a person to normal life

renewable: able to be replaced or restored

representative democracy: a type of democracy, where citizens have the right to choose someone to represent them on a council or in government

respect: to have a good opinion of someone

responsibilities: something it is your duty to do or to look after

retraining: learning new skills that can be used in a different job

road pricing: a scheme which charges road users according to how much they use a road

school council: a group of people who represent the classes and year groups of the school. They give students the opportunity to participate in decision making

Secretary of State: an MP who is in charge of a government department such as health or defence

shadow cabinet: this consists of the leaders of the main opposition party

single currency: this is the Euro, so called as it is used in most of the EU Member States

slander: saying incorrect things about people

small claims court: a local court, which hears civil cases involving small amounts of money

specialized: where employees or businesses concentrate on tasks that they can do well

spin doctor: someone who tries to make bad news sound better

stakeholder: people who have an interest in a decision that is being made

sue: to make a claim against someone or something

sustainable development: living now in a way that doesn't damage the needs of future generations

tolerance: open-mindedness, acceptance

trade unions: organizations that look after the interests of a group of employees

Trading Standards: an official body that enforces consumer-based laws

United Nations: an international organization that tries to encourage peace, cooperation and friendship between countries

ward: an area that forms a separate part of a local council

warnings: written or spoken warnings given by an employer to an employee if the employer thinks the employee has been breaking the contract of employment

White Paper: this puts government policy up for discussion before it becomes law

youth council: a group of young people who meet to discuss what is going on in the local area and put their ideas to the council

Index